The Apricot Affair

Rachel Vdolek

© 2017 Rachel Vdolek

Table of Contents

Introduction 6
A few notes about apricots 7
Apricot Cream Cheese Fruit Dip 9
Apricot Pineapple Salsa 11
Apricot Chili Wings 12
Crispy Shrimp with Apricot Chili Dipping Sauce 14
Apricot Lemonade Iced Tea 16
Apricot Lemonade 19
Apricot Orange White Sangria 20
Apricot Vanilla Milkshake 23
Apricot Strawberry Blueberry Smoothie 24
Apricot Basil Smoothie 26
Apricot Strawberry Milkshake 29
Apricot Daiquiri 31
Apricot Martini 32
Apricot Sunrise 34
Apricot Manhattan 36
Apricot and Chicken Salad with Blackberry Lime Vinaigrette 38
Apricot Orange Poppy Seed Dressing 40
Apricot Chicken Salad 42
Apricot Rice Pilaf 45
Apricot Stuffing 47
Apricot Chili Glazed Salmon 49
Apricot Blueberry Steak Sauce 50

Apricot Chicken Stir Fry 52

Apricot BBQ Sauce 55

Apricot Lime Marinated Shrimp 57

Apricot Coconut Curry Mussels 58

Apricot Teriyaki Burger 60

Apricot Strawberry Crisp 62

Apricot Trifle 65

Apricot Bread Pudding 67

Apricot Sparkling Jello 68

Apricot Muffins 70

Apricot Almond Bread 72

Apricot Scones with Lemon Glazed 74

Biscuits with Stewed Chai Apricots 78

Apricot Coffee Cake 80

French Toast Paninis with Apricot Filling 83

Apricot Chai Spiced Pancakes 84

Vanilla Waffles with Apricot Syrup 86

Crepes with Apricot Jam & Whipped Cream 89

Final Words 91

About the Author 93

Introduction

Apricots are one of those fruits that almost everyone loves. They are so cute and little, but they sure pack a punch of flavor.

My favorite memory of apricots is one with my grandma, or Babi as I called her, which is Czech for grandma. She would always buy me apricot nectar to drink because I loved the stuff. The only time I got to enjoy apricot nectar was when I would visit her house.

She also always had dried apricots that I would love to munch on as a snack, along with cheese cubes, while I was waiting for dinner to be cooked.

When I think of apricots, I think of her and it makes me feel good.

I hope you enjoy these recipes and they make you feel as good as I do when I eat them!

-Rachel

P.S. I'd love to see your photos of my recipes! Follow me on Instagram at Instagram.com/huckleberryeats and tag me or use #huckleberryeats to show off your versions of my recipes!

A few notes about apricots

For the recipes in this book, you will need three apricot staples: fresh apricots, dried apricots and apricot nectar.

Fresh apricots are in season in the summer time and are usually only available for a few short months. Keep your eyes open for apricots starting in mid-May until early August to get the freshest and best ones. Look for ones that are blemish free and not bruised.

Most apricots are picked vastly under ripe and so they will need a few days to ripen. They are ripe when they give slightly to pressure when you squeeze them, but not so much that they get mushy. If they are rock hard, they are under ripe. To quickly ripen them, place them near bananas or apples as these two fruit give off a lot of ethylene gas, which causes fruits to ripen quicker.

Dried apricots come in two types: sulfured and unsulfured. You can tell the difference by their color: the sulfured ones retain their golden orange hue, whereas the unsulfured ones turn brown. You can use either for the recipes and the taste will be the same.

Apricot nectar is the juice of apricots, often combined with other juices, since apricots aren't the juiciest of fruits. Be sure to read the label before buying to make sure you get one with the most apricot juice versus one with lots of pineapple or apple juice. I like Kern's brand, simply because that's what I drank growing up, but it does have HFCS (high fructose corn syrup). If you are avoiding artificial sugars, try an organic brand.

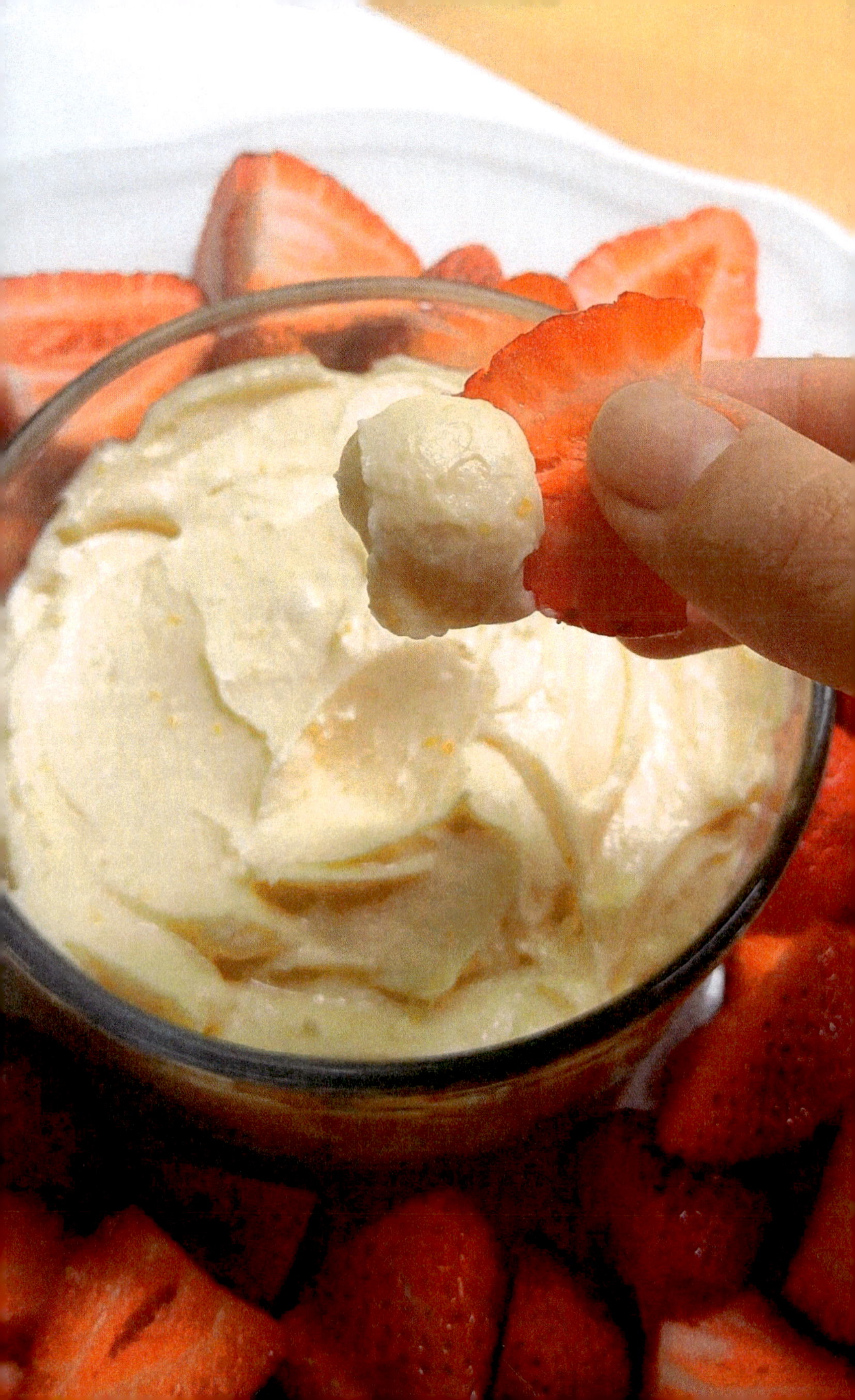

Apricot Cream Cheese Fruit Dip

Serves 8

Time: about 10 minutes

This recipe makes for some really crazy good fruit dip. This spread is also good on toast or English muffins. It's even kid approved! I gave a sample to my cousin for her kids to eat and they gave it two thumbs up!

1 package cream cheese, left at room temp for 30 minutes

4 tbsp apricot preserves

1 tbsp honey

Strawberries, pretzel sticks or apple slices

In a food processor, combine cream cheese, apricot preserves and honey. Pulse to combine, then scrape down. Pulse again a few times until completely blended. If you like it fluffier, continue to blend for another 30 seconds to 1 minute.

Using a spatula, scoop cream cheese mixture into a bowl. Serve with strawberries, pretzel sticks or apple slices.

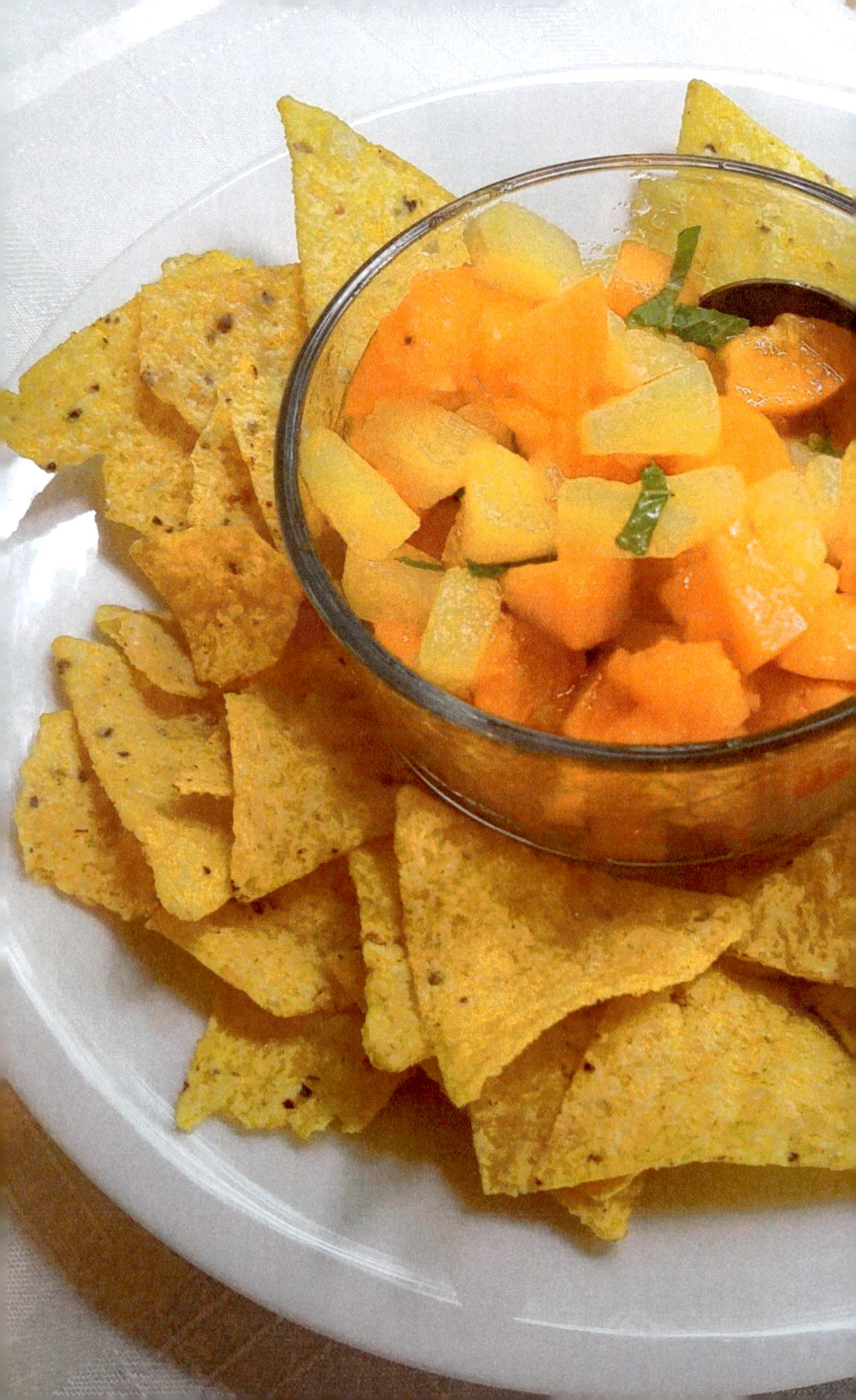

Apricot Pineapple Salsa

Serves 4

Time: 10 minutes

I love fruit salsas. They are so different from regular salsas that it makes it fun! This one is no exception. It's really easy to make. Plus its nice and sweet but a little tart. Its great with tortilla chips or cinnamon sugar pita chips, but I loved it on chicken tacos with grilled peppers. Simply season some chicken thighs with taco seasonings, cook chicken until done, then chop up meat. Heat up some tortillas, then top with chicken, sliced grilled peppers and top with salsa. Add a bit of hot sauce if you like and enjoy!

2 apricots, diced

1/2 can pineapple tidbits

1/8 tsp dried ginger

2 mint leaves, finely sliced

Combine ingredients in a bowl, then let stand for 10 minutes. Serve with tortilla chips or cinnamon sugar pita chips.

Or serve on chicken tacos!

Apricot Chili Wings

Serves 8

Time: 2 hours

I love wings! I used to stick to the standard Buffalo sauce, but then I started making my own, so you know I HAD to experiment. This is hands down the best wing sauce I've made so far. It's not too spicy but it's sweet and sticky and oh so good. Feel free to add more chili paste if you like your wings hot.

1 lb wings, frozen

1/4 c. apricot preserves

1/4 c. water

1 tsp garlic chili paste

Spread wings, still frozen, on a baking sheet. Bake at 400 F for about 15 minutes, then lower heat to 350 F. Bake for another 30 minutes, then drain juices from pan. Return wings to oven for a final 15 minutes or until desired crispiness.

To make sauce, combine all ingredients in a saucepan, then heat over low heat until preserves melts and the sauce becomes smooth. Let simmer for 10 minutes then when wings are done, toss wings in sauce. Put wings back onto sheet pan, then toss back into the oven for 5 minutes to let the sauce get sticky!

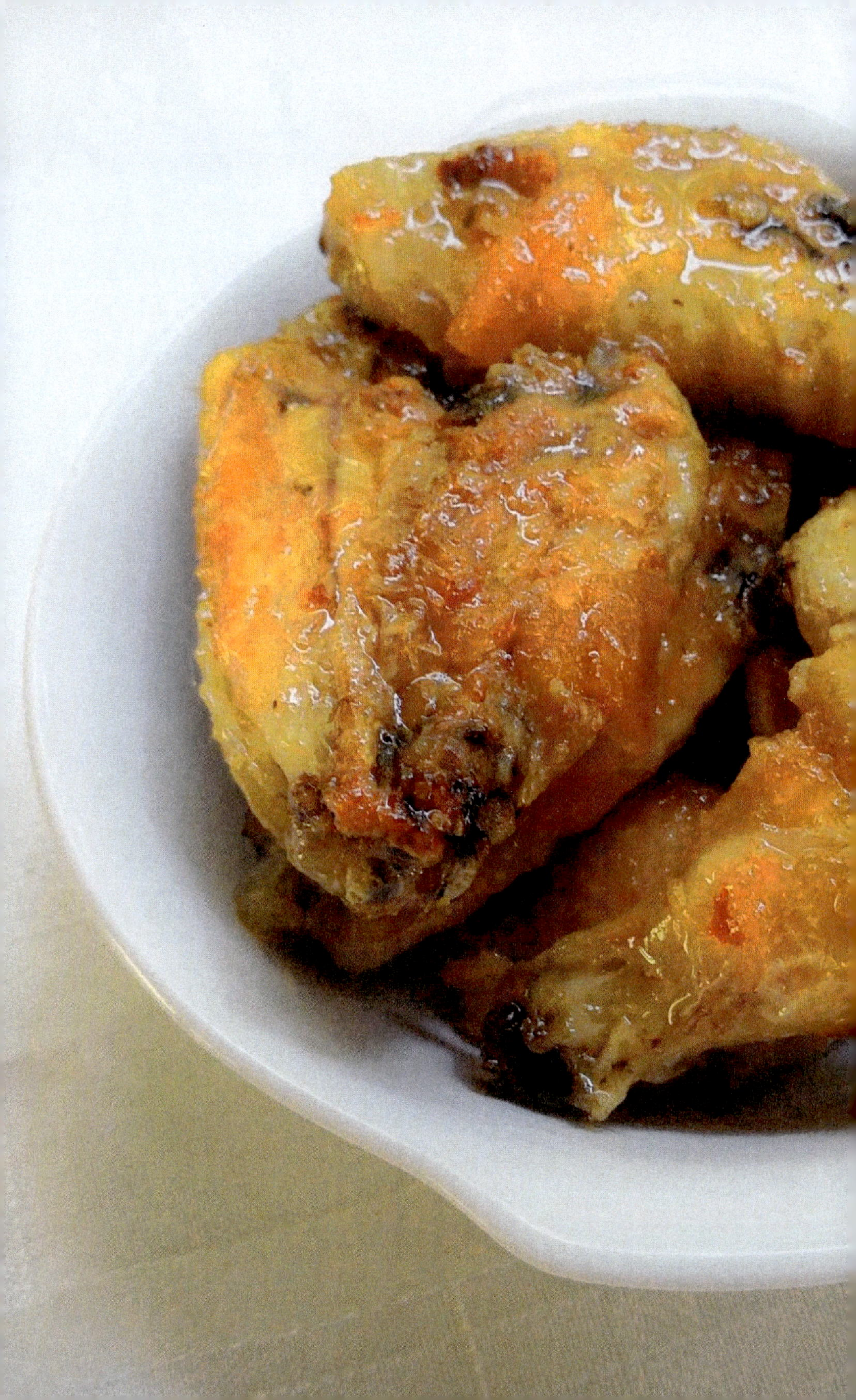

Crispy Shrimp with Apricot Chili Dipping Sauce

Serves 4

Time: about 30 minutes

I am a sucker for crispy shrimp. Anywhere I go, if there are tempura shrimp or deep fried shrimp, I've got to try them. Usually, I just prefer cocktail sauce or a sweet and sour sauce, but this one takes the cake. It's sweet but spicy and of course, creamy! At home, I like to use a Louisiana fish fry mix to coat the shrimp because it's light but crispy. I also shallow fry them so they are just a smidge healthier.

About 2 dozen jumbo shrimp, peeled and deveined

Louisiana fish fry mix

Vegetable shortening

Sauce:

1/4 c. mayonnaise

2 tbsp apricot preserves

1 tsp sriracha (more if desired)

To make sauce, stir together all ingredients. Set aside to let flavors meld.

To make the shrimp, pat shrimp dry, then toss in Louisiana fish fry mix.

Add a few scoops of shortening to a saute pan, then melt shortening over medium heat. Add a few shrimp (don't crowd the pan) and let cook for 1-2 minutes per side. Once shrimp are crispy and curled up, remove from pan onto a paper towel lined plate. Repeat to cook all shrimp. Serve with the sauce for dipping.

Apricot Lemonade Iced Tea

Makes 4 drinks

Time: 10 minutes plus chilling

I've never been a fan of Arnold Palmers until a major coffee chain started making them. (Hint: I'm from Seattle and the chain is from there too!) Now I'm addicted. My favorite is a passion tea lemonade but this one is just as refreshing, without the added sugar. It's super easy to make and as long as you have the ingredients on hand, it comes together quickly.

2 black tea bags

2 c. water

1 1/2 c. apricot nectar

1 c. lemonade

Bring water to a boil, remove from heat and add tea bags. Steep for 5 minutes, then set aside to cool. Refrigerate for at least 1 hour before using.

To make a drink, combine 1/2 c. black tea, 1/2 c. apricot nectar and 1/4 c. lemonade. Stir then enjoy.

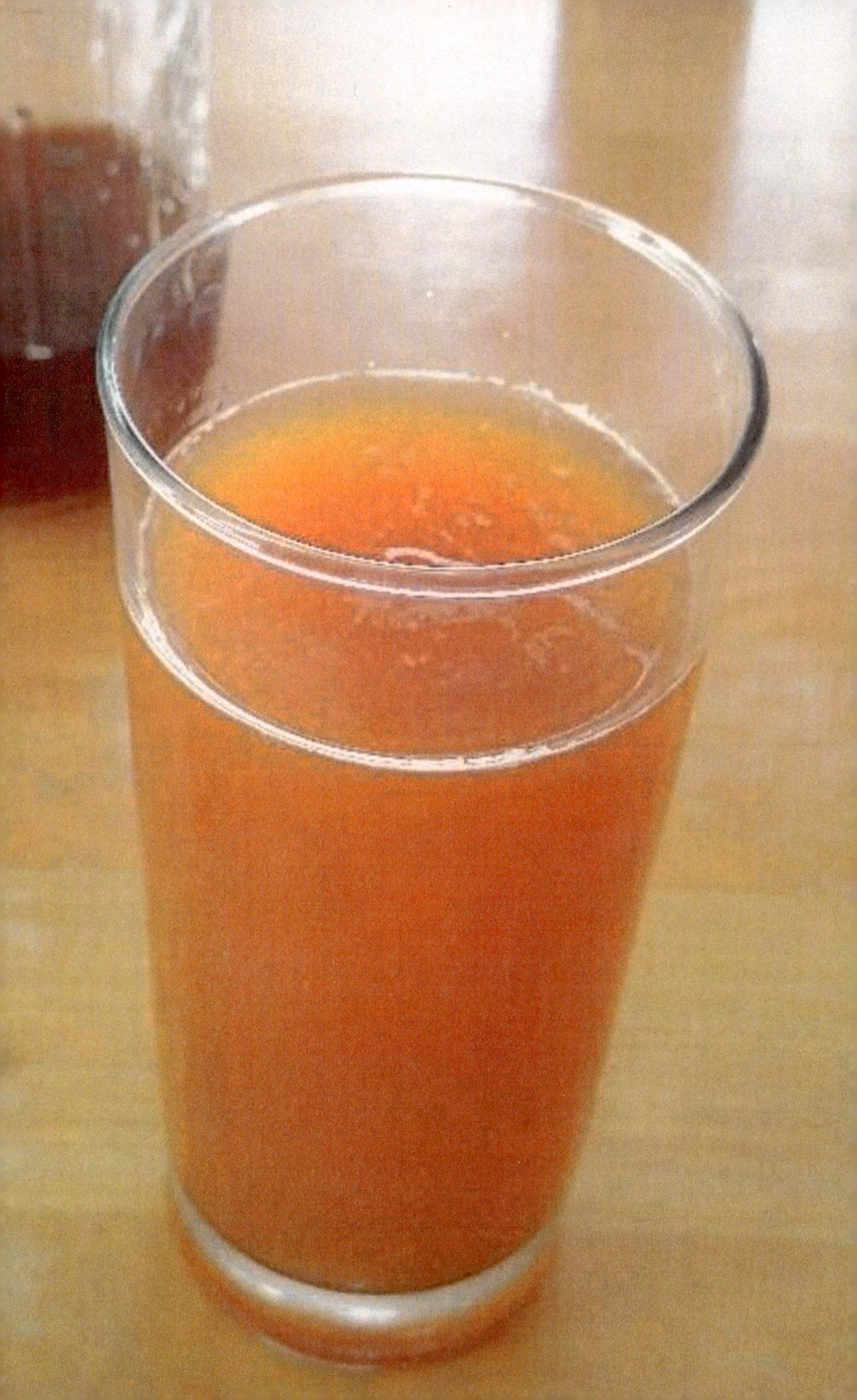

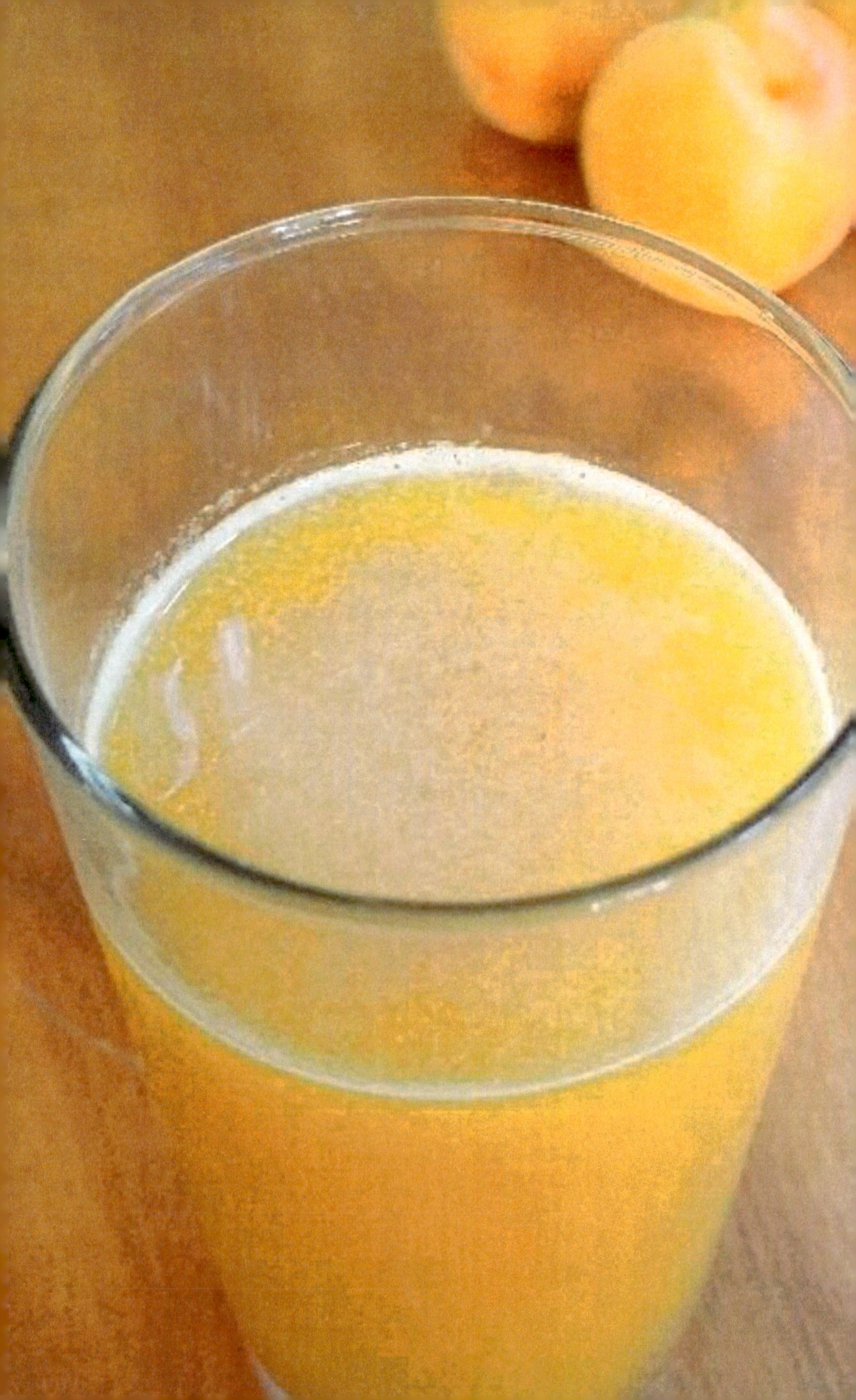

Apricot Lemonade

Makes 2 drinks

Time: about 5 minutes

Lemonade is the perfect summer drink. It's light but sweet and almost impossible to improve. Unless you add in some apricot nectar. The sweet tartness of the nectar pairs so well with the lemonade. If you are looking for a nice alternative to regular lemonade, this is it.

1 1/2 cups lemonade

1 1/2 cups apricot nectar

In a large pitcher, combine lemonade and apricot nectar. Stir to combine, then serve over ice.

Apricot Orange White Sangria

Serves 4

Time: 10 minutes plus marinating

I love sangria, but I prefer a white sangria over the red. For any sangria, you want to pick a wine that you would drink plain. So if you love sweet whites, you won't want to pick a dry one for this. I love Pinot Gris (also known as Pinot Grigio) and it works really well in this sangria because it's not super sweet but not super dry. It's also usually got hints of citrus already in there, so it's practically perfect in this drink. Just keep in mind, the longer you let the fruits marinate, the stronger the fruit flavor will be.

3 cups white wine

1 apricot, pitted and sliced

1/2 can mandarin orange slices, drained

1/4 cup apricot nectar

1/4 cup orange juice

In a large pitcher, combine all ingredients. Stir to combine, then refrigerate at least 2 hours and up to 2 days. Serve in large wine goblets and sit out on the deck to relax.

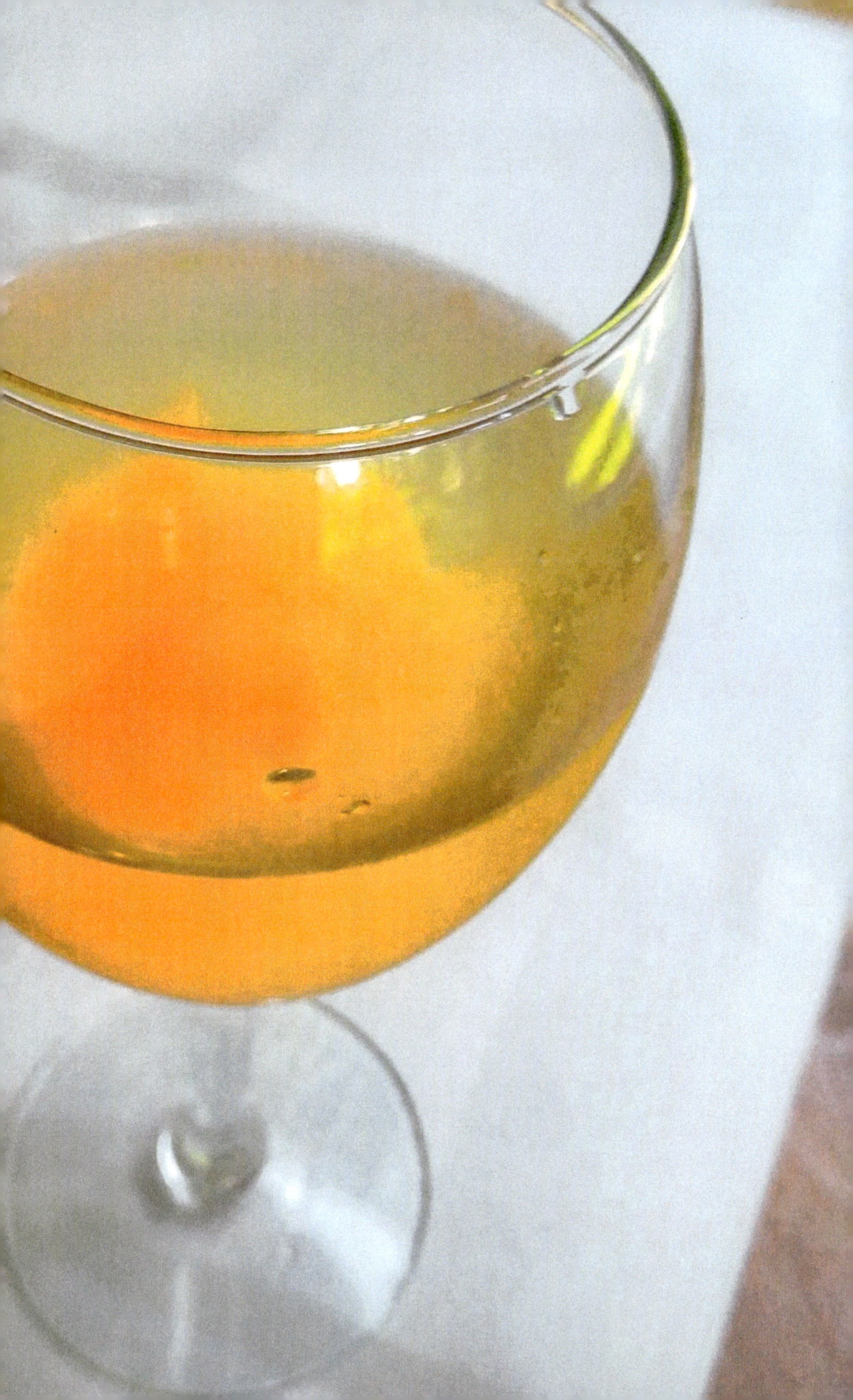

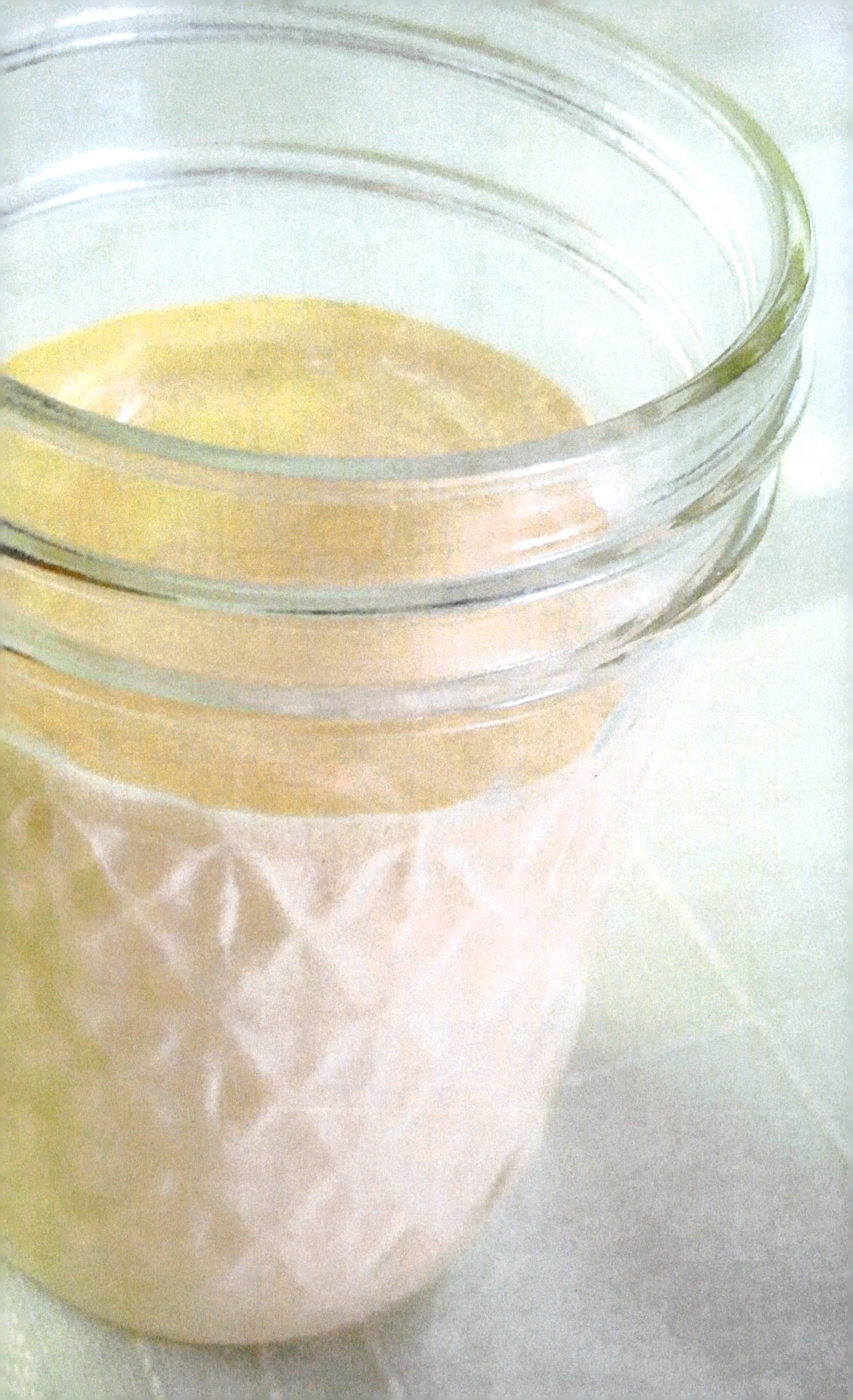

Apricot Vanilla Milkshake

Serves 1

Time: 5 minutes

To be honest, I'm not the biggest fan of milkshakes. I never really grooved on them to much until college, but even then I pretty much stuck with chocolate. Until I had this one! It's tangy and sweet, but not too sweet, like most milkshakes are. If you like yours a little on the runny side, feel free to add more milk.

1 scoop vanilla ice cream

1/2 cup milk

1 apricot, cut in half and pitted

Combine all ingredients in a blender. Blend until smooth. Add a little sugar if you like your milkshakes sweeter.

Apricot Strawberry Blueberry Smoothie

Serves 1

Time: 10 minutes

Smoothies are the perfect breakfast or after workout snack. They go together quickly and you can mix and match ingredients and make them different each time. This one is no exception. You can add in some kale to get your daily greens in, or add in ginger and turmeric for anti-inflammatory goodness. Or leave it as is for a Vitamin C punch!

1 apricot, cut in half and pitted

1/2 c. blueberries

3 strawberries, hulled and cut in half

1 banana

Orange juice

In a blender, combine all ingredients. Add orange juice just to cover fruit, then blend until smooth.

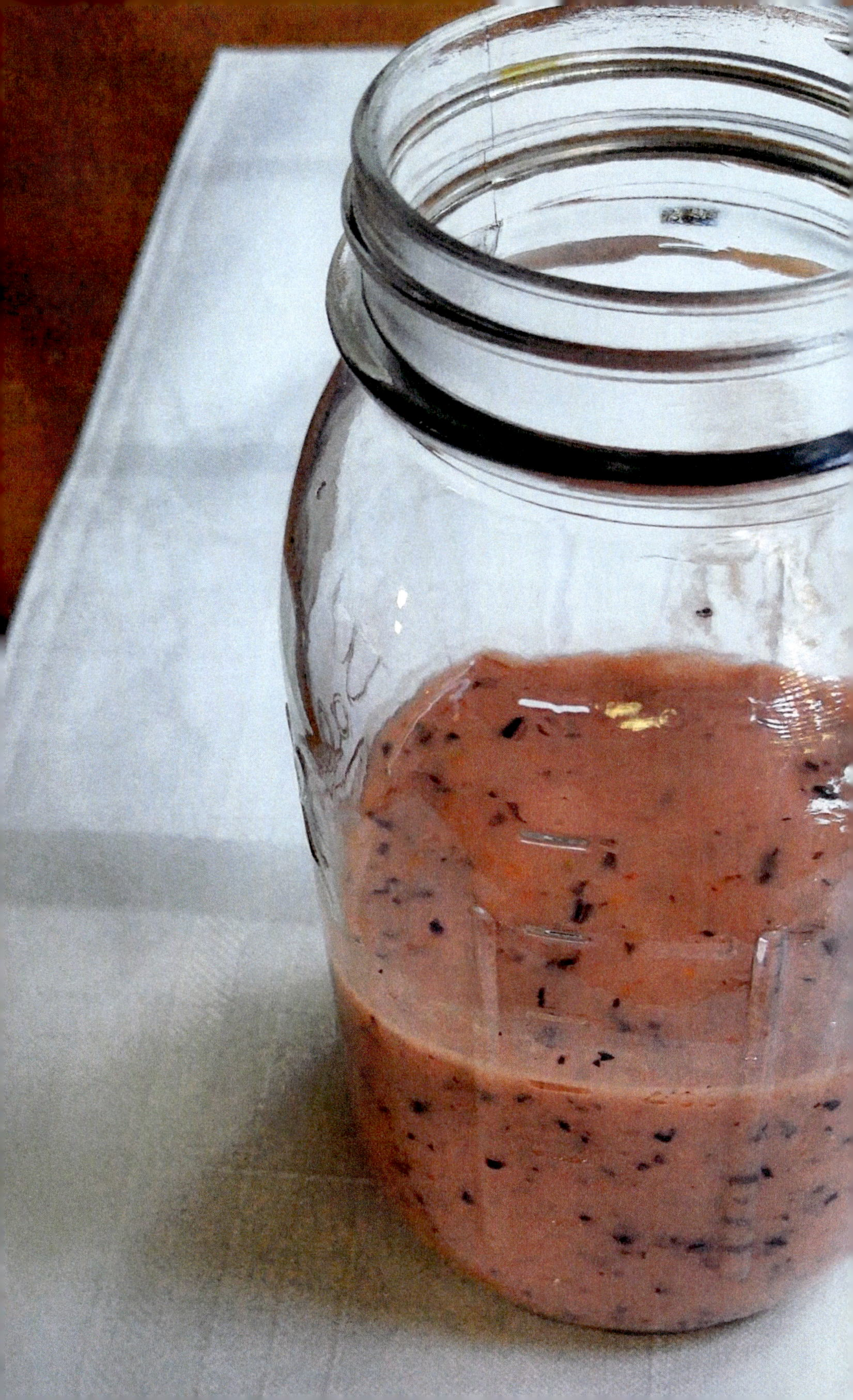

Apricot Basil Smoothie

Serves 1

Time: 10 minutes

Sometimes fruit smoothies are good as is, other times you want something creamy, almost milkshake-y, but still healthy. This is that one. The apricots are a bit tart on their own, so if you want it on the sweeter side, be sure to add in some honey or agave to sweeten it, or use sweetened almond milk.

1 apricot, cut in half and pitted

4 basil leaves

1 banana

Unsweetened almond milk

Honey or agave, if desired.

In a blender, combine all ingredients. Add in enough almond milk to cover fruit, then blend until smooth.

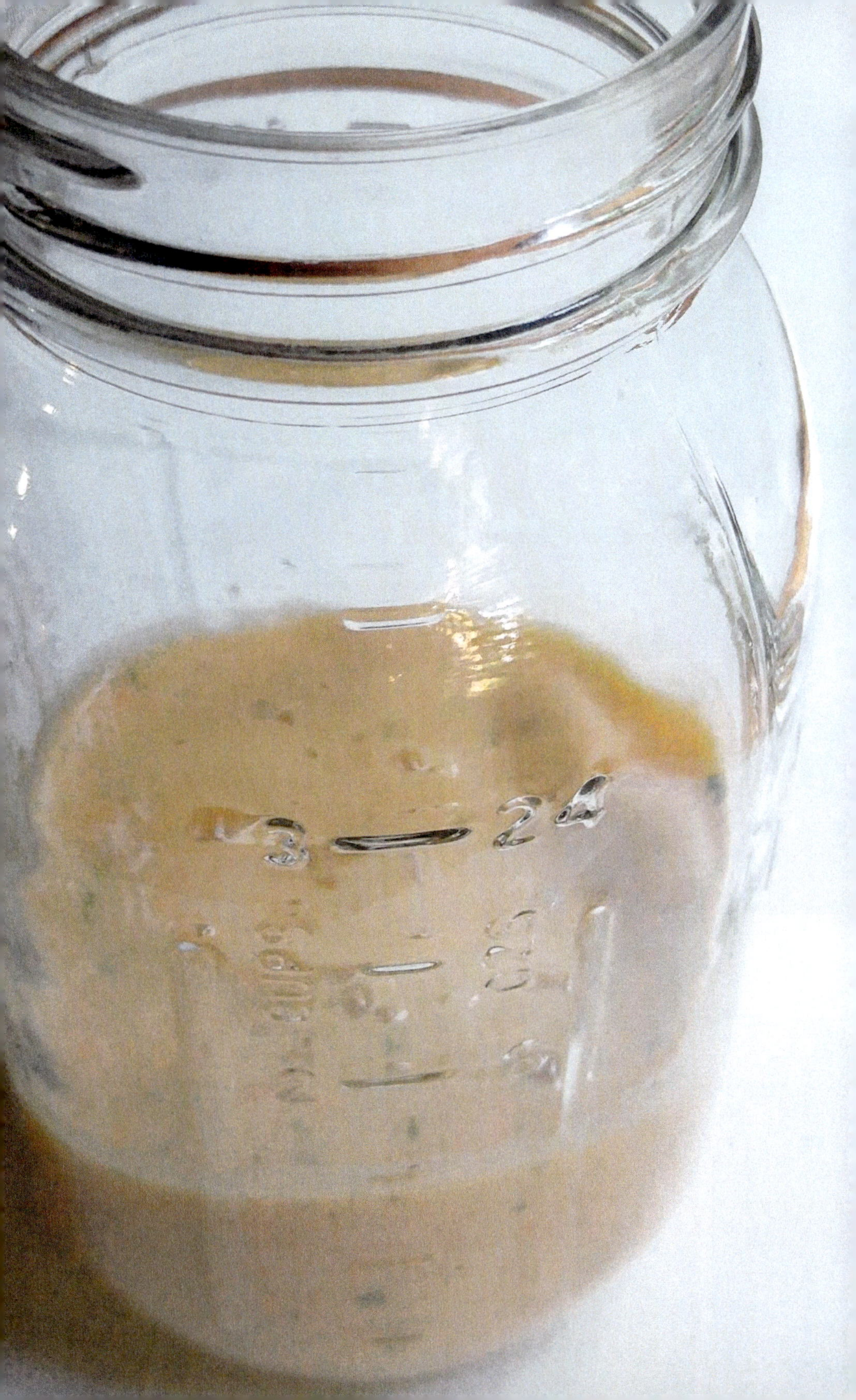

Apricot Strawberry Milkshake

Serves 2

Time: 10 minutes

This is another milkshake recipe that really hit it out of the park! The apricots and strawberries go so well together, plus the vanilla ice cream adds some sweetness too! If you happen to get a batch of fruit that is a bit on the tart side (like mine was!), feel free to add some honey or sugar to sweeten it up.

2 apricots, cut in half and pitted

6 strawberries, hulled

1/2 cup milk

2 scoops vanilla ice cream

Combine all ingredients in a blender, blend until smooth.

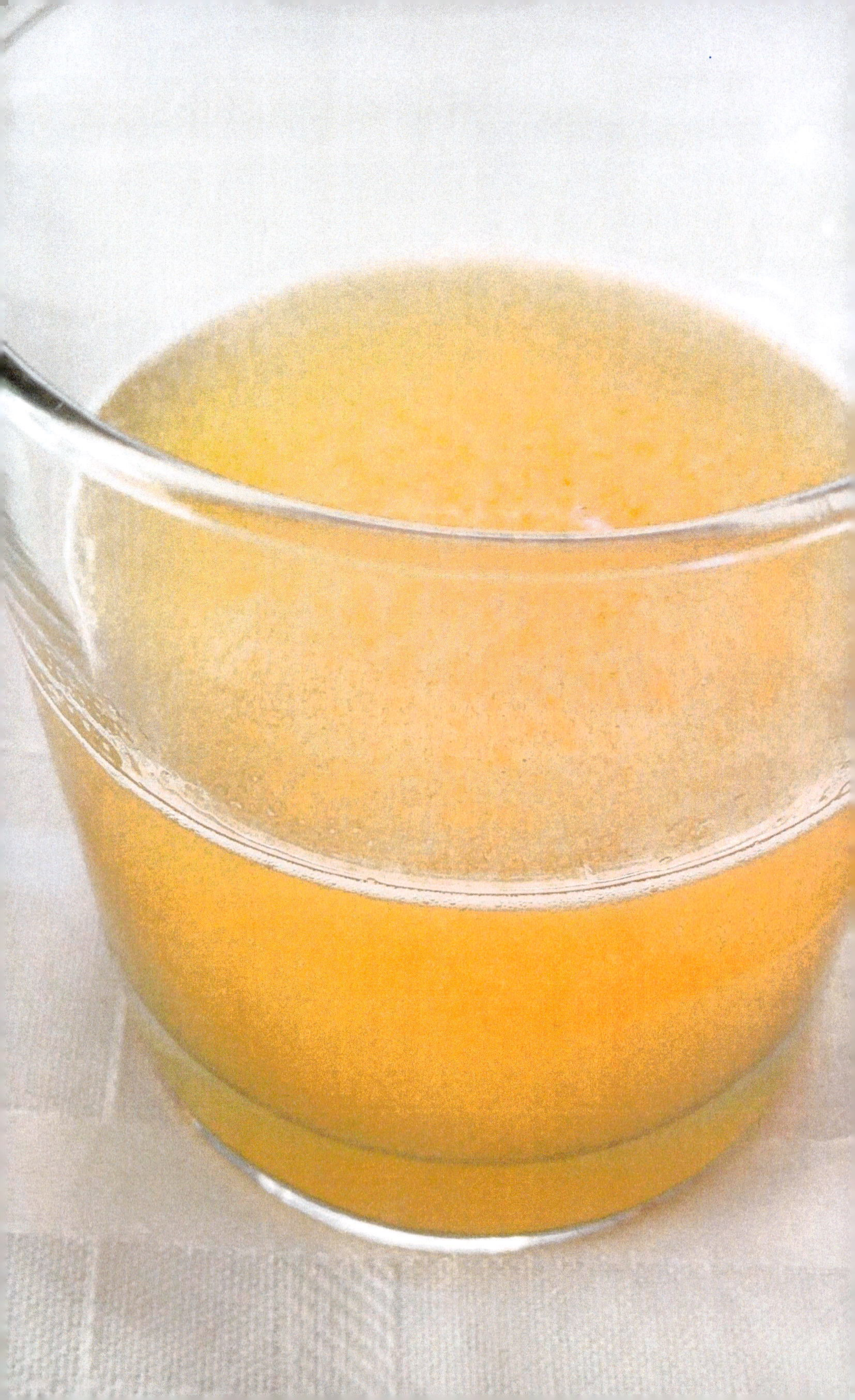

Apricot Daiquiri

Makes 1 drink

Time: 10 minutes

If you like your drinks tart, this is the one for you. It's really really tart, but its also very refreshing. I loved it, and so did one of my taste testers, but another one said it was too sour. If you like your drinks on the sweet side, simply reduce the lime juice to 1/2 oz and increase the simple syrup to 1 oz.

1 1/2 oz. rum

1/2 oz. simple syrup

1 oz. apricot nectar

1 oz. lime juice

Combine all ingredients in a cocktail shaker with a few cubes of ice. Shake, then strain into a glass.

Apricot Martini

Makes 1 drink

Time: 10 minutes

This martini was probably the best drink of the bunch. It's sweet but delicious and super easy to make. The hint of lemon really enhances the apricot flavor, but if you prefer the taste of vodka, simply reduce the apricot nectar to 1 oz.

2 oz vodka

1 1/2 oz apricot nectar

1/2 oz simple syrup

2 strips of lemon peel

Combine all ingredients except 1 of the strips of lemon peel in a cocktail shaker with a few cubes of ice. Shake, then strain into a glass. Add the 2nd strip of lemon peel to the glass for garnish.

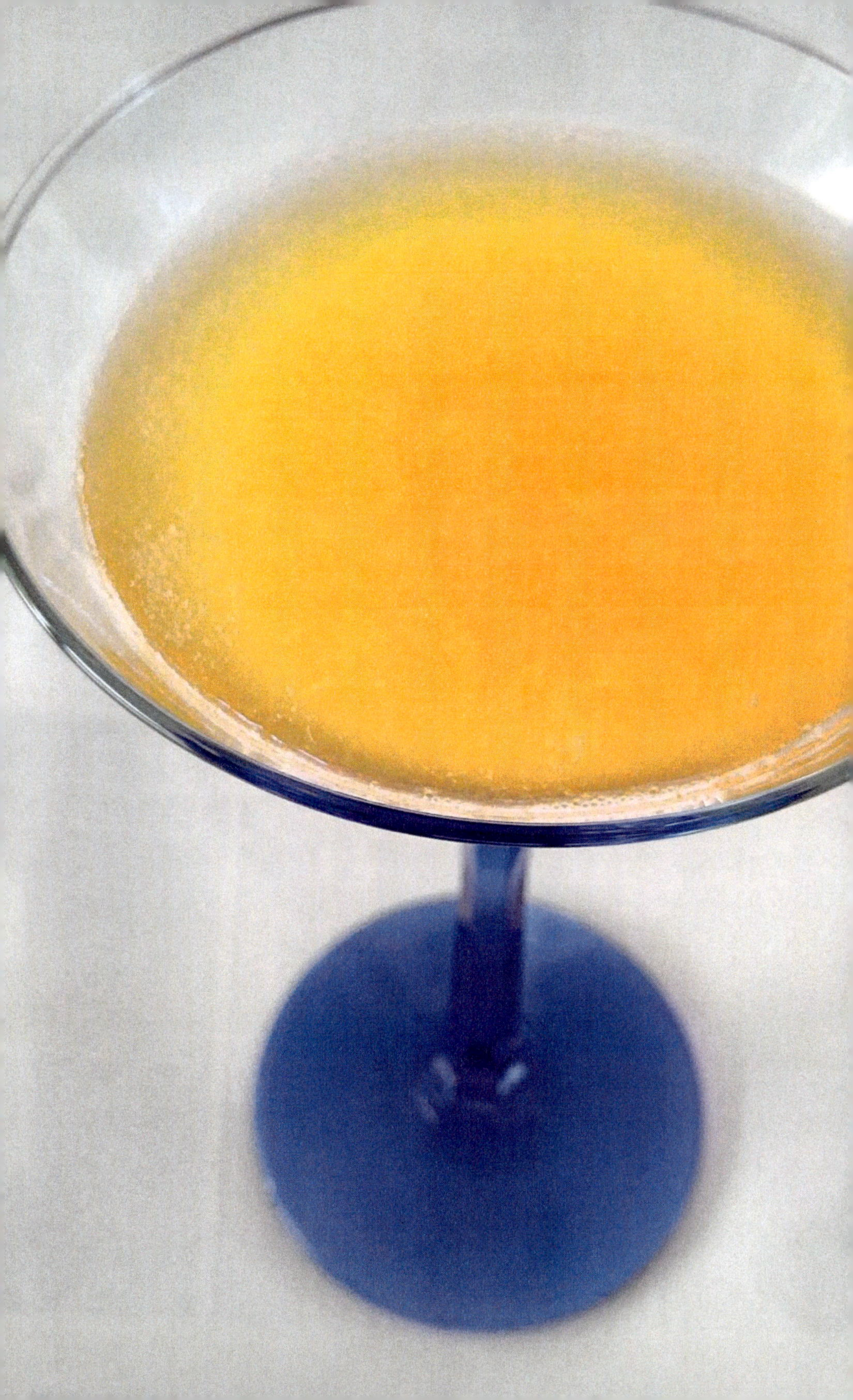

Apricot Sunrise

Makes 1 drink

Time: 10 minutes

I'm a huge fan of tequila sunrises. They are one of my favorite drinks. So why not add a hint of apricot to it? It was definitely refreshing on a hot day!

1 oz apricot nectar

1 oz orange juice

1 oz tequila

1/2 oz grenadine

Combine first three ingredients in a cocktail shaker with a few cubes of ice. Shake, then strain into a glass. Top with grenadine syrup.

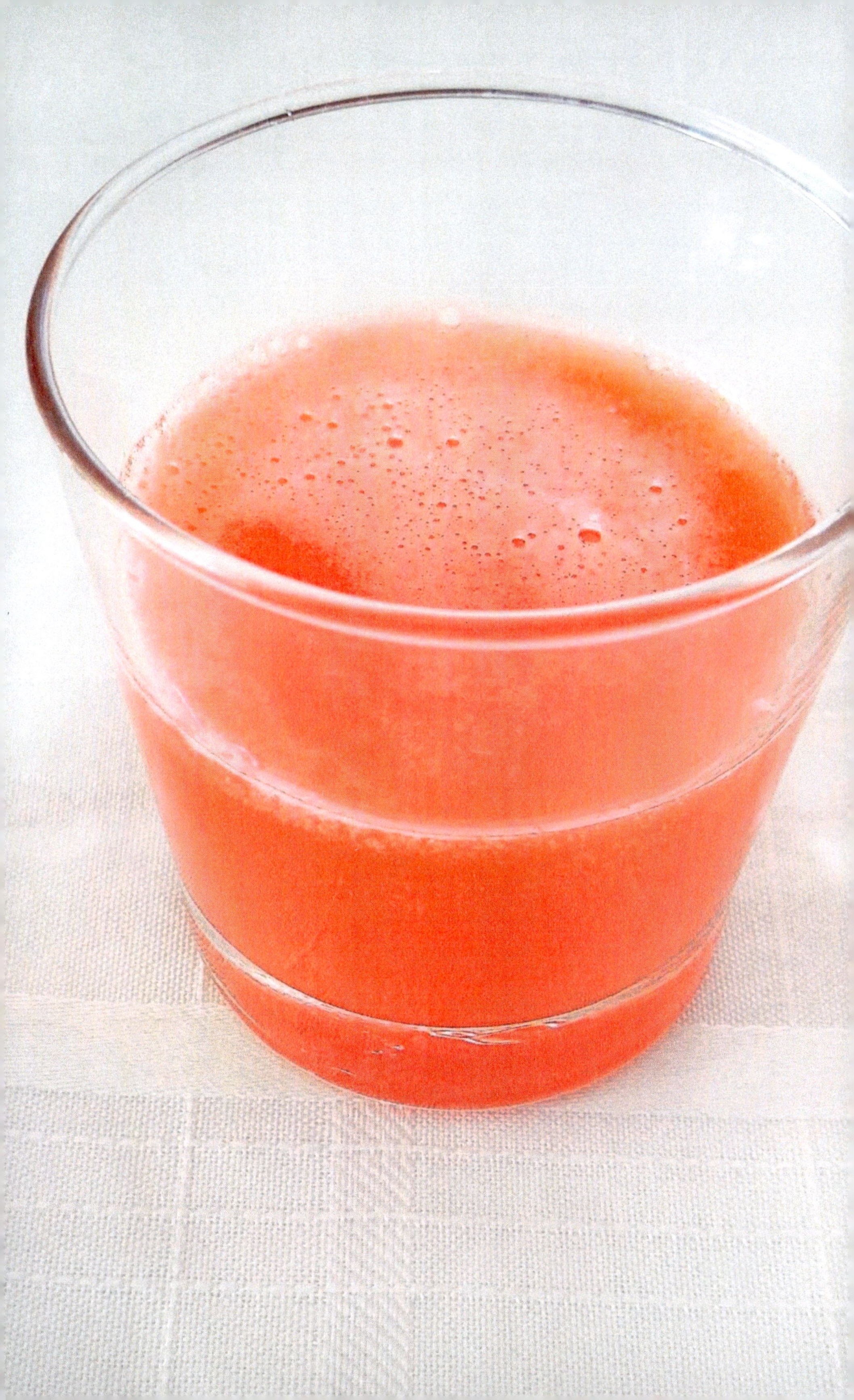

Apricot Manhattan

Makes 1 drink

I had only tried a Manhattan once or twice before I went to this Italian restaurant near my house and they were featuring a cherry Manhattan. While it was way too sweet for me, it gave me the idea to make an apricot one! And this one was definitely a hit!

2 oz whiskey

3/4 oz sweet vermouth

1 oz apricot nectar

1/2 oz simple syrup

Dash of Angostura bitters

Maraschino cherries

Combine all ingredients except cherries in a cocktail shaker with a few cubes of ice. Shake, then strain into a glass. Add a few cherries for garnish.

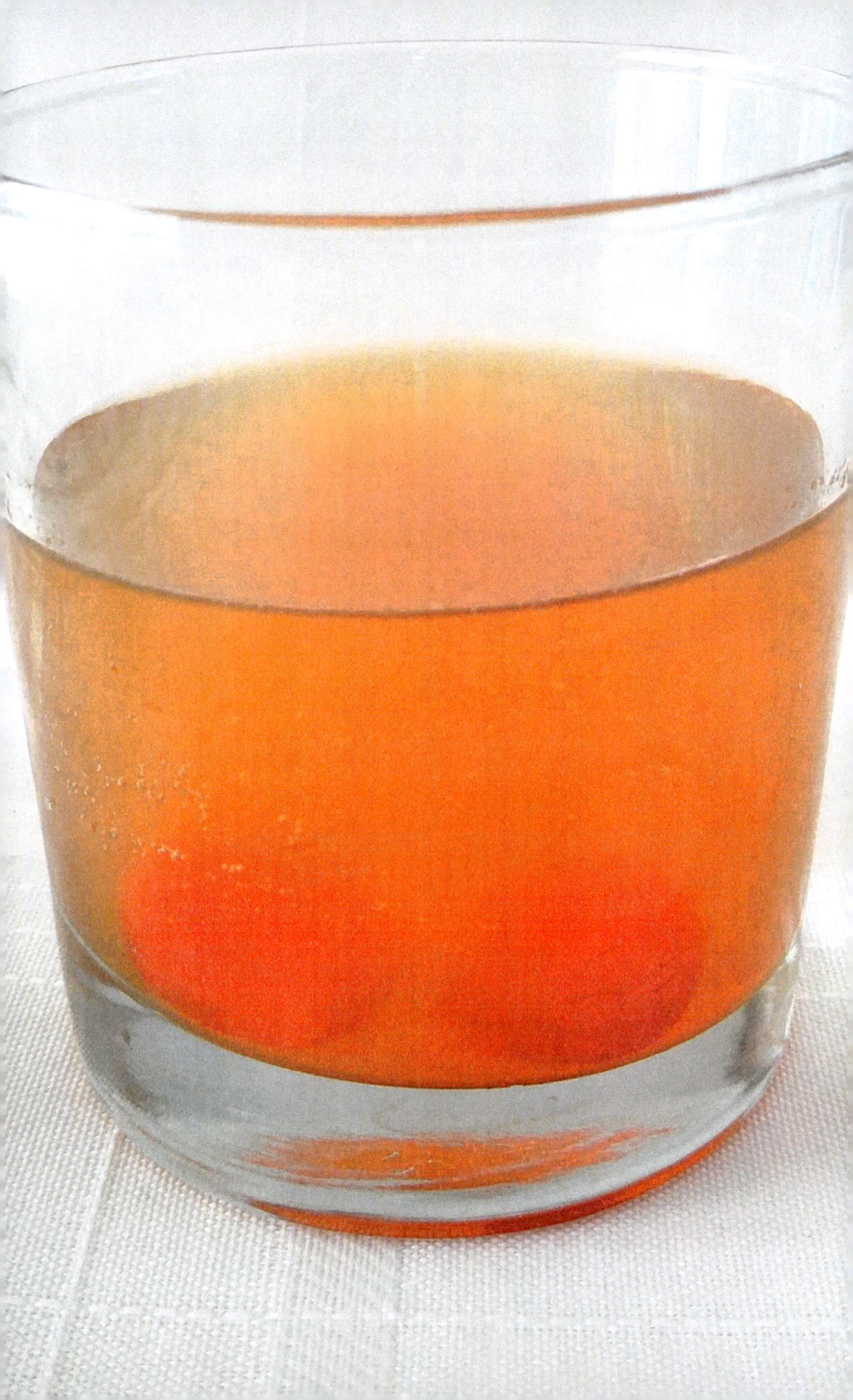

Apricot and Chicken Salad with Blackberry Lime Vinaigrette

Serves 4

Time: about 30 minutes

Fruit in salads always makes me happy. I don't know what it is, but I love a little pop of sweetness in a salad. This one has a double pop since it has apricots and blackberries. Plus its got some great crunch from the veggies and the nuts. This is one of my new favorite salads!

2 boneless skinless chicken breasts

2 tbsp butter, softened

4 leaves parsley, chopped

4 chives, chopped

1 sprig thyme, stem removed

1/4 tsp garlic salt

4 apricots, sliced

4 dates, sliced

1/4 c. chopped almonds

2 celery ribs, diced

1 cucumber, peeled and diced

Salad greens

Dressing:

1/4 c. blackberries

Juice from 1/4 lime

1/4 c. champagne vinegar

1 tbsp honey

1/2 c. canola oil

1/4 tsp salt

1/8 tsp pepper

To make dressing, combine ingredients in a blender. Blend until emulsified, then strain into a bowl through a metal strainer. Use a spoon to stir the dressing through the strainer. Set aside.

In a small bowl, combine butter, parsley, chives, thyme and garlic salt. Stir to combine. Cut each chicken breast in half lengthwise to create two 1/2" thin tenders. Heat a grill pan over medium high heat, then grill chicken breasts. Cook on one side for about 3-4 minutes, then flip. Spread butter on the cooked sides and let it soak into the chicken. Cook on the second side for another 3-4 minutes, or until fully cooked. Remove from heat, let cool, then thinly slice.

To assemble salad, place a handful of greens on each plate. Sprinkle apricot slices, dates, almonds, celery and cucumber over the top. Add one chicken piece over each salad, then drizzle with dressing.

Apricot Orange Poppy Seed Dressing

Makes 1 c. of dressing

There is this one salad blend that I cannot get enough of. It's got kale, Brussels sprouts, cabbage and plenty of other hearty greens. It comes with a standard poppy seed dressing, which I love! For some reason the sweet dressings go really well with the heartier greens. And this apricot one is no exception! I enjoyed it on a salad with grilled chicken, almonds and bell peppers and it was delicious!

1/2 c. apricot nectar

1/4 c. mayonnaise

1/4 tsp salt

1 tbsp orange juice

1 tsp honey

1/4 c. vegetable oil

1 apricot, cut in half and pitted

1 tsp poppy seeds

In a blender, combine all ingredients except poppy seeds. Blend until smooth. Stir in poppy seeds then serve on salad greens.

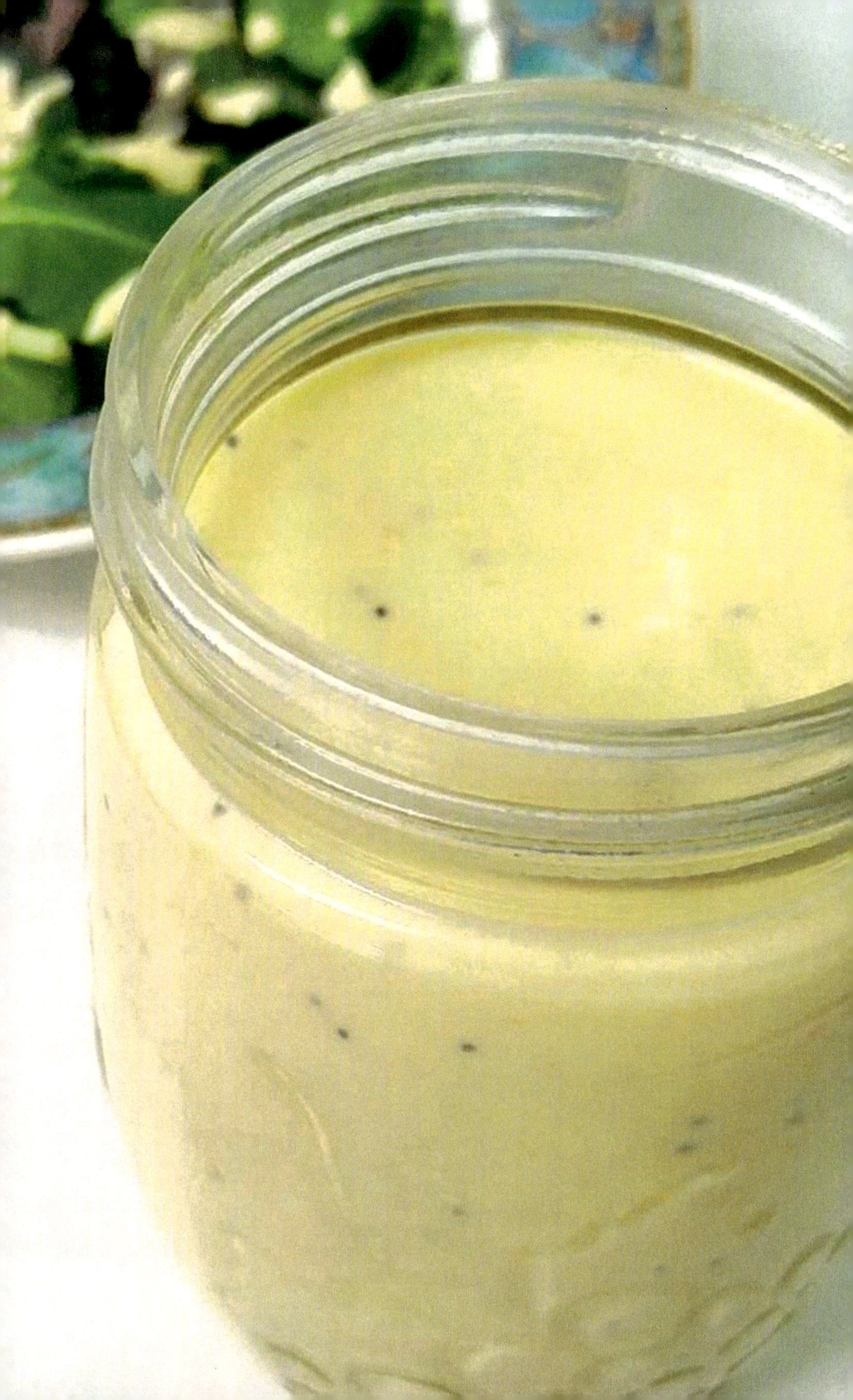

Apricot Chicken Salad

Serves 4 as sandwiches or on a salad

Time: about 30 minutes

I never used to like chicken salad very much until I started making it for myself. I love to add in yummy mix-ins like dried cranberries and chopped almonds. This one is my favorite now because the dried apricots plump up from the mayo and turn into a nice little sweet tart contrast to the creamy chicken salad. Toss in some almonds for some crunch and you have one awesome sandwich! Even one of my friends who hates chicken salad said he loved this one!

2 boneless skinless chicken breasts

Oil

Garlic salt

2 ribs celery, finely diced

1/2 onion, finely diced

1/4 c. slivered almonds, chopped

8 dried apricots, finely chopped

1/4 c. mayonnaise

To cook chicken, split chicken breasts lengthwise to create four 1/2" thick pieces. Rub each piece with oil and sprinkle with garlic salt. Heat a non-stick pan over medium high heat, then add chicken breasts. Cook for 3-4 minutes on each side until thoroughly cooked. Remove from heat and set aside to cool.

Once chicken is cooled, chop into a small dice. Combine chicken, celery, onion, almonds and apricots in a large bowl. Add in mayonnaise and stir to combine. Feel free to add more mayonnaise if you prefer.

Serve on bread as a sandwich or on top of salad greens.

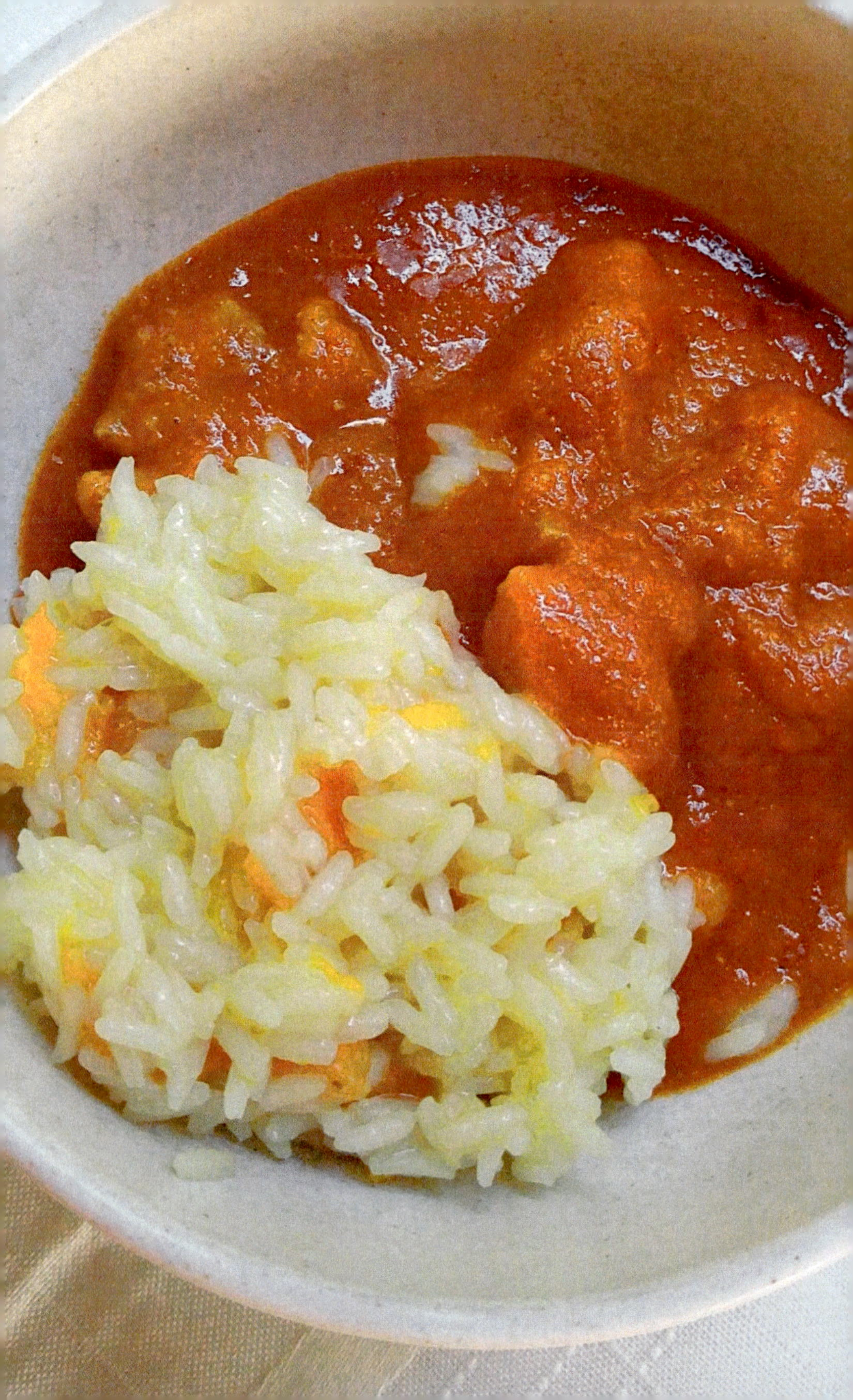

Apricot Rice Pilaf

Serves 4

Time: 20 minutes

Rice can be kinda bland if you don't add extra stuff in. This one packs a huge flavor boost with the dried apricots and makes it a great pairing to any spicy dish. I served it with an Indian chicken curry to help cool it down, but this rice pilaf would be great with grilled meat and a salad, too.

1 c. rice

2 1/2 cups chicken broth

1/4 tsp ginger

1/4 tsp garlic salt

6 dried apricots, chopped

In a medium saucepan, heat chicken broth to a boil. Add in rest of ingredients, then reduce heat to low. Simmer for 15 minutes until rice is cooked. Leave off heat to stand for 5 minutes to absorb rest of the liquid, then serve.

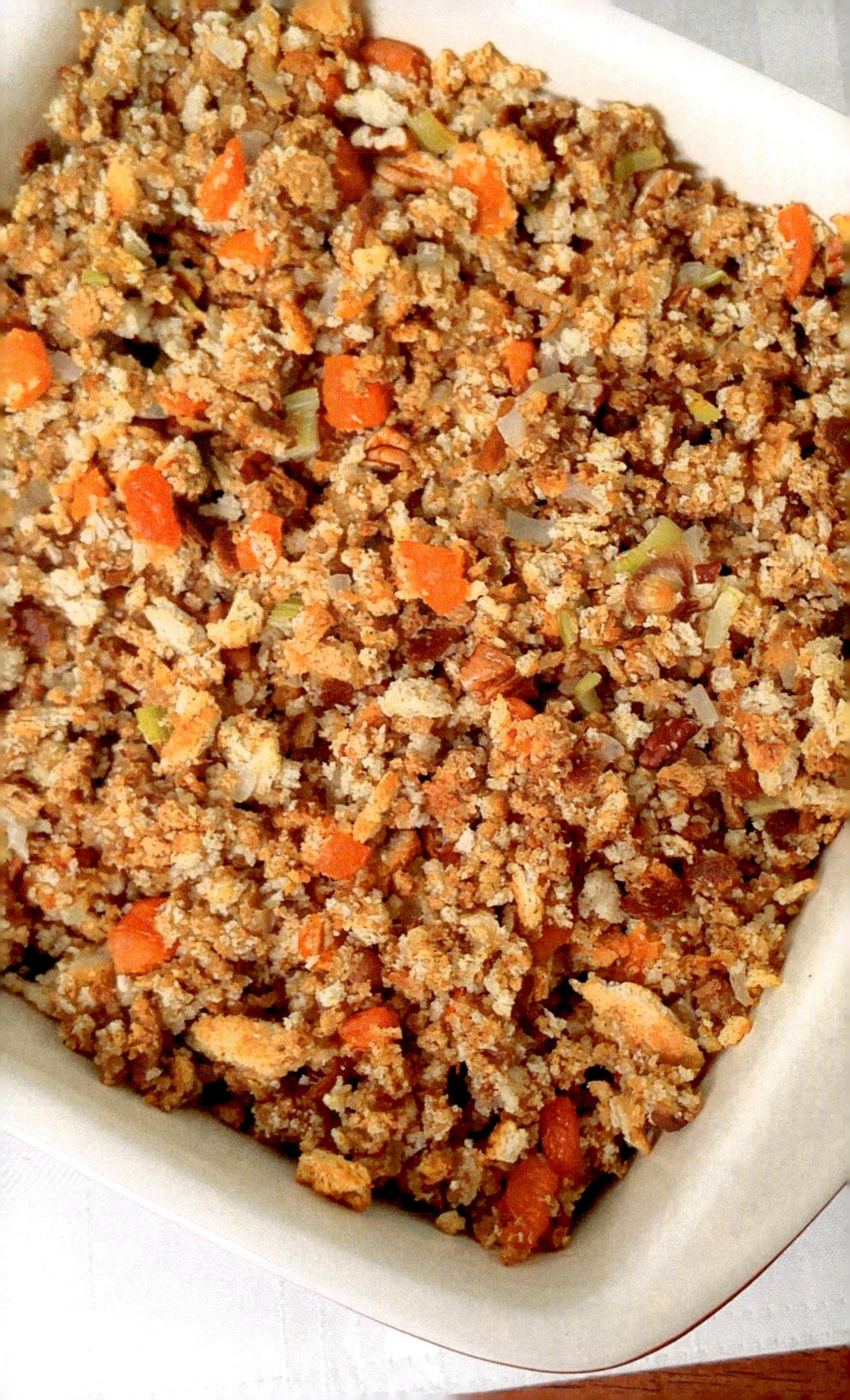

Apricot Stuffing

Serves 4

Time: 1 hour

In my opinion, stuffing is great anytime of the year. Why wait for Thanksgiving to enjoy it? This is a great fresh twist on the traditional version that adds just a pop of color and sweetness to an already awesome dish. Be honest, I know you think the stuffing is the best part of Thanksgiving anyways!

10 dried apricots, diced

2 celery stalks, diced

1 onion, diced

5 tbsp butter

2 cups chicken stock

1/4 tsp thyme

1 package herb seasoned stuffing mix

Add dried apricots to chicken stock. Let soak until ready to use.

Heat butter in a large saute pan. Add onion and celery and cook until translucent, but not brown. Add in thyme and chicken stock, then stir in stuffing mix. Keep stirring until moistened. Add extra chicken stock if needed to moisten.

Pour stuffing mix into a baking dish, then cover with foil. Bake at 350 F for 20 minutes, then remove foil and bake for last 10 minutes uncovered.

Alternatively, stuff a turkey with stuffing and enjoy!

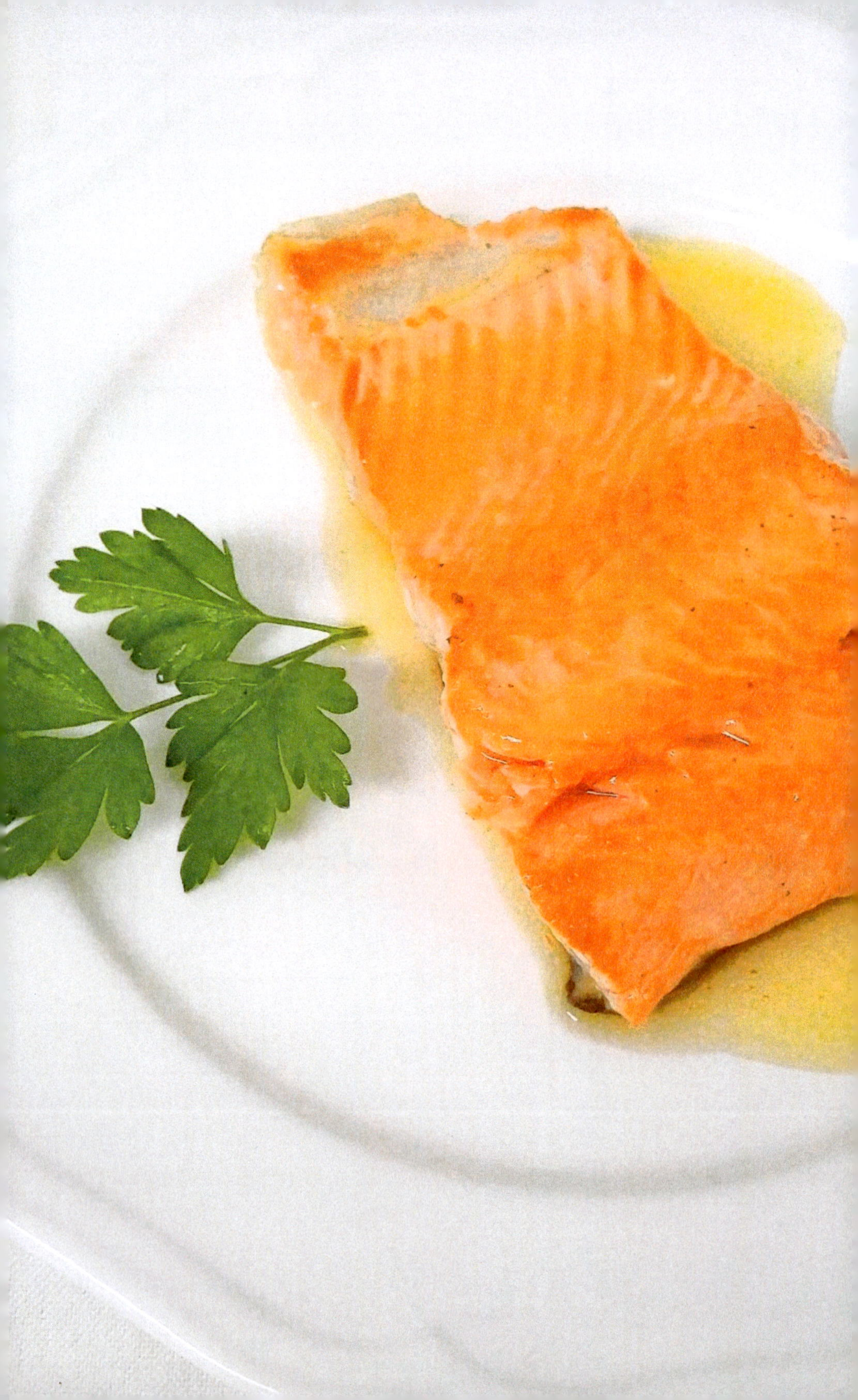

Apricot Chili Glazed Salmon

Serves 4

Time: 20 minutes

I'm a sucker for glazed salmon. One of my favorites is a simple combo of teriyaki sauce, brown sugar and butter, but this apricot one takes the cake. If you like your food spicy, feel free to add more sriracha.

1 lb salmon fillets	1 tsp sriracha
2 tbsp butter	Garlic salt
2 tbsp apicot preserves	Parsley, for garnish

In a small saucepan, combine apricot preserves, butter and sriracha. Bring to a simmer, then stir til combine. Remove from heat and set aside.

Cut salmon into 4 pieces. Sprinkle with garlic salt. Heat a non-stick pan over medium heat, then add salmon, skin side up. Sear salmon for 2-3 minutes until salmon lifts from pan easily. Flip over and cook for another 2-3 minutes, or until salmon is done.

Spoon apricot glaze on top and let cook for one more minute to set glaze. Serve with a sprinkling of chopped parsley.

Apricot Blueberry Steak Sauce

Serves 4

Time: about 1 hour

I'm a huge fan of sweet sauces with steak. One of my favorite steak sauces is a fig with sweet onions, but this one is better. The apricot and blueberries make the sauce a little sweet but not too overpowering. Be sure to let the sauce rest off the heat for a while to let the flavors mellow together, otherwise it may be a bit on the tomato-y side. Trust me, the wait is worth it.

1 tbsp oil

1/4 onion, finely diced

1/4 c. blueberries, rinsed and drained

2 apricots, finely diced

2 cups of beef stock

1/4 c. dry sherry

1 tsp tomato paste

1/4 tsp garlic salt

Heat a medium saucepan over medium heat. Add oil, then onions. Cook onions for 3-4 minutes until lightly browned and translucent. Add in remaining ingredients, bring to a simmer and cook for 20 minutes, uncovered.

Pour the sauce into a blender and blend until smooth. Return to saucepan and simmer for 20 more minutes, uncovered. Set aside to cool and let the flavors mellow for a final 20 minutes before serving over your favorite cut of steak.

Apricot Chicken Stir Fry

Serves 4

Time: 30 minutes

Stir fries are my go-to dinners. They come together quick and are super healthy, not to mention tasty. I usually stick to my standard sauce, but this one is by far the best stir fry I've ever made. It reminds me of sweet and sour chicken, just not battered and deep fried. So basically, it's healthier!

1 lb. chicken thighs, cut into bite sized pieces

1/4 tsp garlic salt

2 carrots, peeled, thinly sliced

2 celery stalks, sliced on a bias

1 yellow bell pepper, cored and diced

1 clove garlic, minced

Vegetable oil

Sauce:

1/4 cup pineapple juice

1/4 cup apricot nectar

1/4 cup teriyaki sauce

1 tsp lemon juice

1/8 tsp fresh grated ginger

2 tbsp cornstarch

Combine all ingredients for sauce together in a bowl, let stand while cooking.

Heat a large saute pan over high heat. Add 1 tbsp vegetable oil, then add in chicken. Sprinkle with garlic salt, then cook until chicken gets crispy and is cooked thoroughly. Remove chicken from heat, then add in 1 tbsp more oil. Add in garlic, cook for 30 seconds or until fragrant then add in carrots and celery. Cook for 2 minutes. Add in bell peppers, cook for another minute.

Add chicken back into pan. Stir sauce to make sure cornstarch is dissolved then pour into pan. Stir chicken and veggies until sauce is thickened, the immediately remove from heat. Serve over rice.

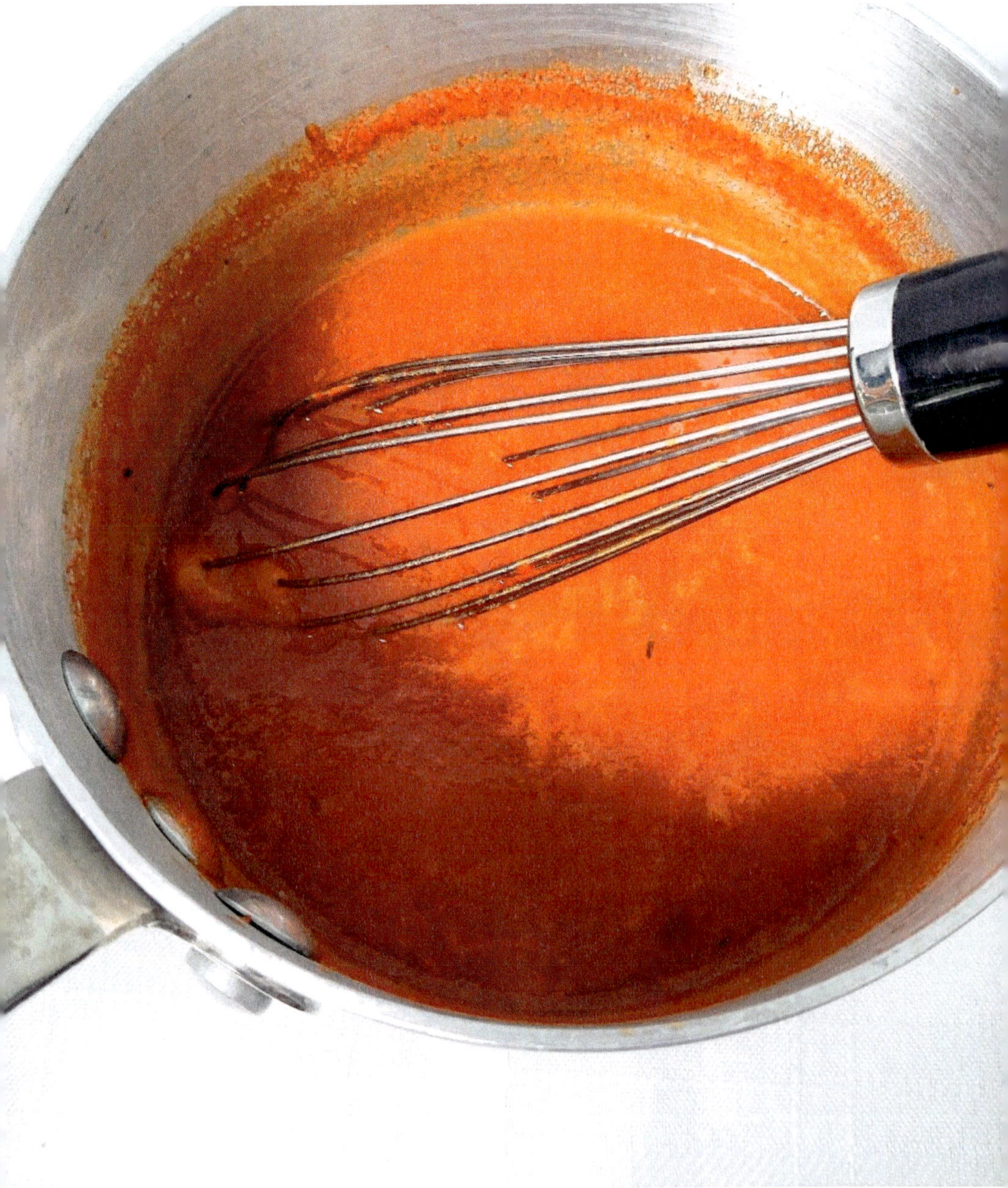

Apricot BBQ Sauce

Makes 1 cup of sauce, enough for 2 lbs of meat

Time: 20 minutes

Apricot in BBQ sauce may not seem like the most normal thing to do, but trust me, it's delicious! The apricots bring a nice sweet tang to the sauce and its perfect on grilled chicken. I even used it on baked chicken drumsticks and it was delicious for that too! It would be good with wings, ribs, basically any kind of meat, it's really that good.

2 apricots, pitted and diced	1/2 tbsp honey
1/2 cup ketchup	1 tsp Worcestershire sauce
1/4 cup water	1/4 tsp onion powder
2 tbsp finely diced onion	1/8 tsp garlic salt
2 tbsp white wine vinegar	

Combine all ingredients in a saucepan. Bring to a boil, then reduce to a simmer. Cook for 15 minutes, then set aside to cool.

Baste on grilled chicken or ribs during last 5 minutes of cooking.

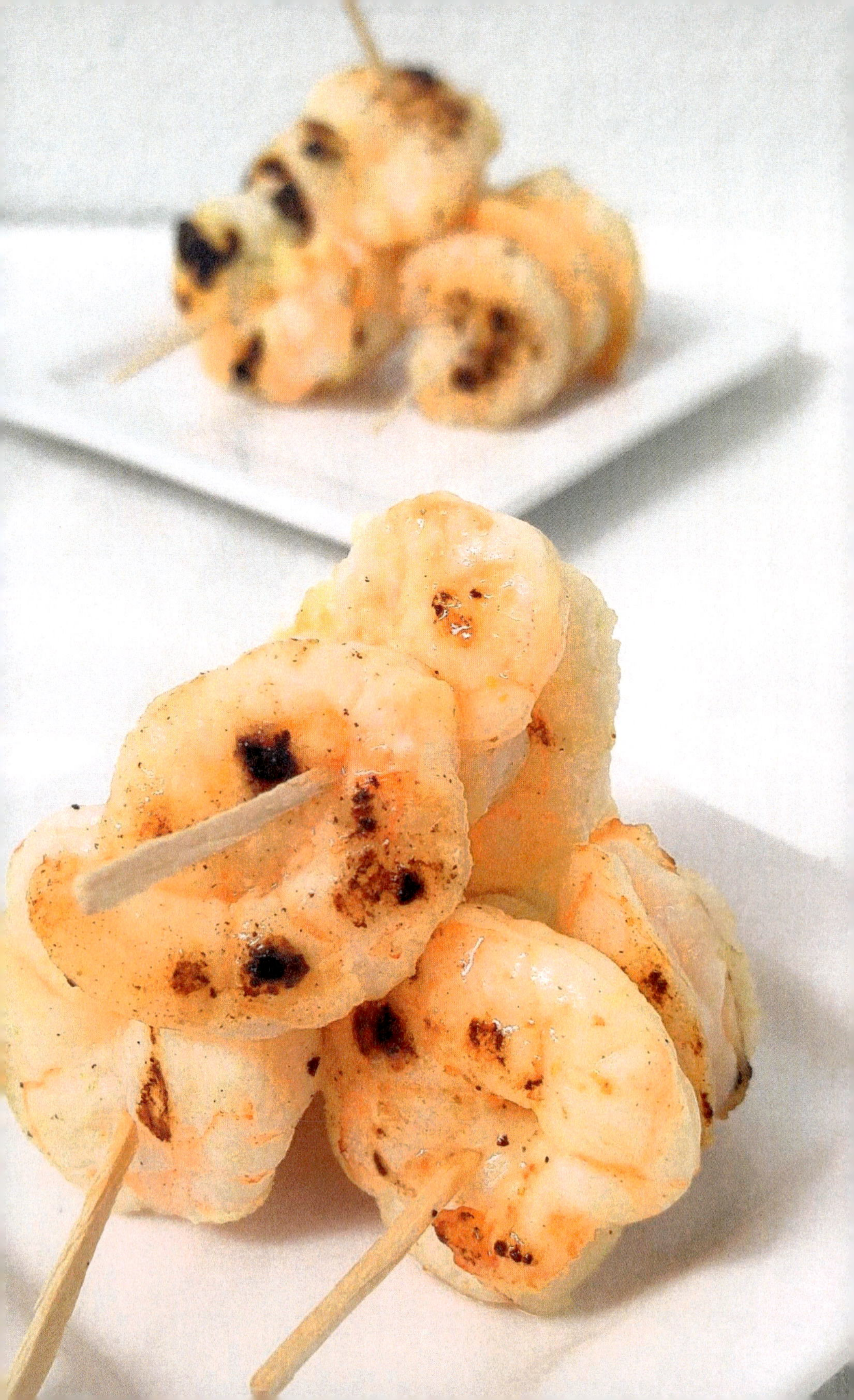

Apricot Lime Marinated Shrimp

Serves 4

Time: 30 minutes plus marinating

These little shrimp were so good I wanted to keep eating them! They make a great little appetizer or are amazing with some stir fried veggies and rice for a simple dinner. Either way, these are a hit!

1 lb raw shrimp, peeled and deveined

Juice of 1 lime

1/2 c. apricot nectar

1/2 c. coconut milk

1 tsp curry powder

1/4 tsp salt

Vegetable oil

Combine lime, nectar, coconut milk, curry powder and salt in a large bowl. Add shrimp and let marinate for 15 minutes at room temperature or up to 1 hour in the refrigerator.

Drain shrimp and pat dry. Heat 1 tbsp vegetable oil in a large saute pan over medium high heat. Add shrimp and saute for 3 minutes, turning over halfway through. Serve hot.

Apricot Coconut Curry Mussels

Serves 4

Time: 30 minutes

I love coconut curry mussels. Something about the curry and the briny mussels just goes so well together. My favorite version is at a restaurant in Seaside, OR but these come mighty close. The apricot adds just a hint of sweetness that makes them extra delicious. Be sure to get some good rice or bread to mop up all that sauce!

1 lb mussels, cleaned and debearded

2 tbsp green curry paste

1 c. coconut milk

1/4 c. apricot nectar

1/4 tsp salt

1 tbsp oil

In a large stock pot, heat oil over medium heat. Add curry paste and cook for 1 minute, until fragrant. Add in coconut milk and apricot nectar. Bring to a boil, then reduce to a simmer. Add salt and mussels. Cook for 8 minutes or until all the mussels have been opened. Discard any that do not open. Serve with rice or bread for dipping.

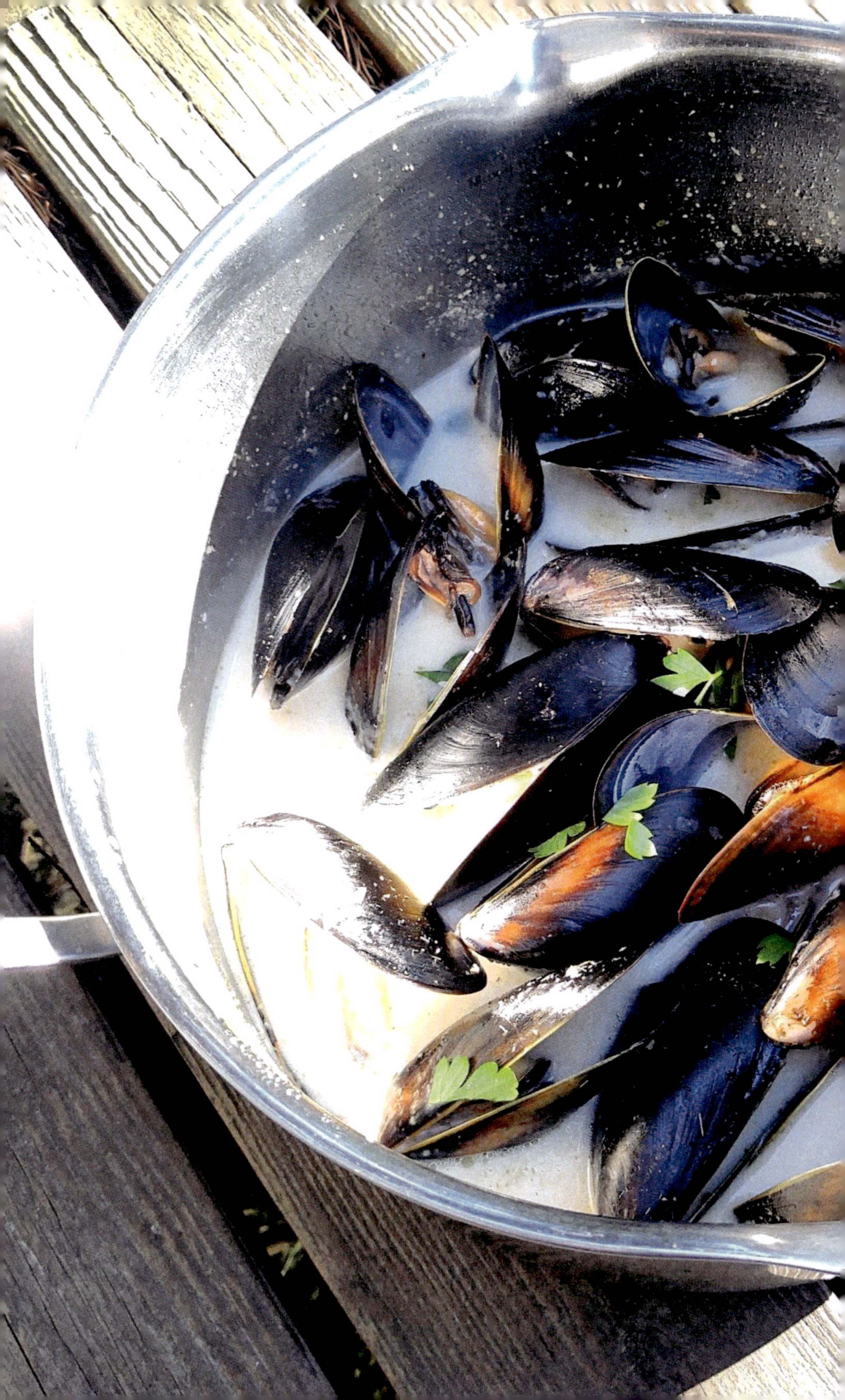

Apricot Teriyaki Burger

Makes 4 burgers

Time: 30 minutes

I knew I wanted to make a burger for this book, but I struggled with what to make for a while. Then it hit me! I should make a teriyaki burger with apricot in the sauce! And man it was a brilliant idea. I ate like 3 of these the week I made it because it was so good! I bet you will want to eat that many too after trying this recipe.

Sauce:

1/4 c. teriyaki sauce

2 tbsp pineapple juice

1 tbsp apricot preserves

2 tbsp pineapple tidbits

2 tbsp water

1 tsp cornstarch

Sriracha mayo (mix together mayo with a few squirts of sriracha or use store bought)

4 colby jack cheese slices

Thinly sliced walla walla onions

Lettuce

4 hamburger buns

4 burger patties

To make sauce, combine teriyaki sauce, pineapple juice, apricot perserves and pineapple tidbits in a small saucepan. In a separate bowl, whisk together water and cornstarch. Bring ingredients in saucepan to a boil, then add cornstarch mixture. Whisk until thickened, then set aside.

Cook burgers however you like to cook them, and top with Colby jack slices. Spread sriracha mayo on burger bun, add burger, then top with sauce. Add lettuce and onion, then add top bun.

Apricot Strawberry Crisp

Serves 4

Time: about 1 hour

Crisps are my favorite dessert to make. They are so simple and easy, yet so delicious. Plus, since it's mostly fruit, I like to tell myself its healthy. Add a scoop of ice cream or a dollop of whipped cream to make it extra indulgent! If you like the topping, feel free to double the topping ingredients for extra crunch.

4 apricots, pitted and sliced

2 cups strawberries, hulled and cut in half

2 tbsp sugar

1/2 cup rolled oats

1/2 cup light brown sugar

1/4 cup all purpose flour

1/4 tsp ginger

1/4 cup butter

Preheat oven to 375 F. Place fruit in a 2 quart square baking dish. Sprinkle with sugar. In another bowl, combine oats, flour, brown sugar and ginger. Cut in butter until mixture resembles coarse crumbs. Sprinkle over fruit.

Bake for 30 to 35 minutes or until topping is golden brown.

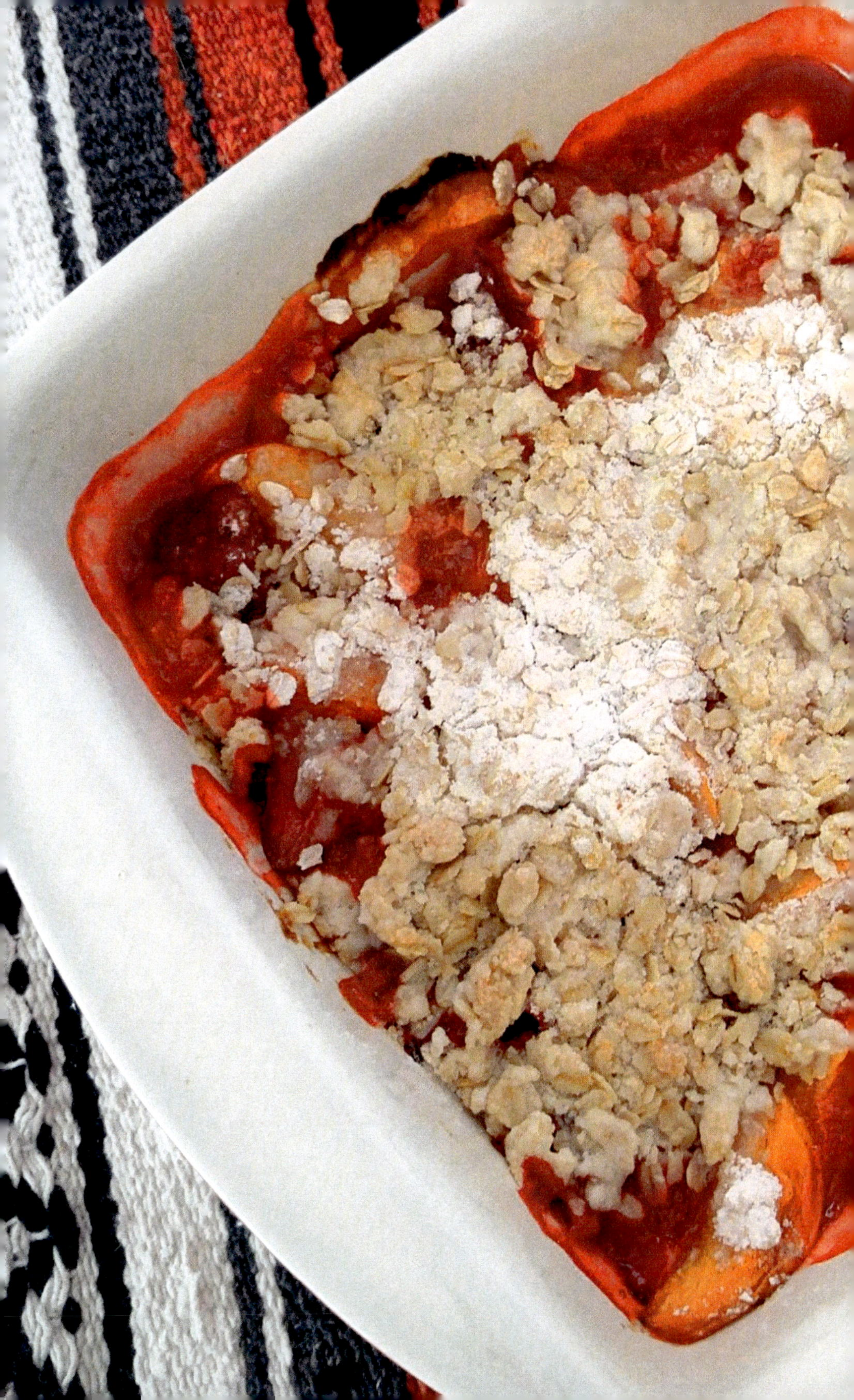

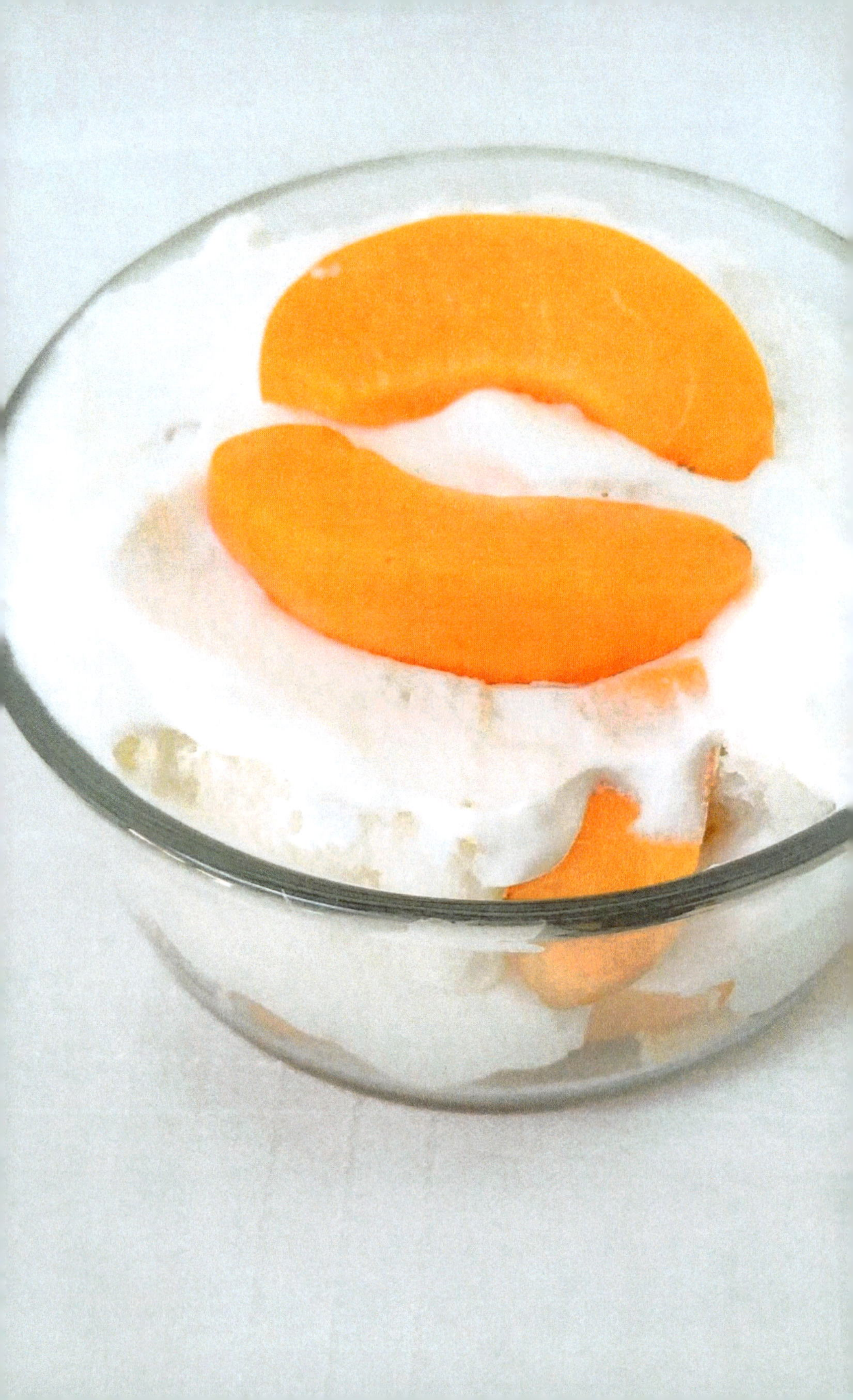

Apricot Trifle

Serves 4

Time: 10 minutes

I love trifles. You don't see them being served as dessert too much in the US, and that's a real shame since they are so easy yet so good! I used store bought angel food cake for mine, but if you want to bake your own cake, feel free to! I prefer making my own whipped cream, but if you like store bought, that's great too. Just as long as it has the main components, you can make it your own as much as you would like.

4 apricots, pitted and sliced

Angel food cake

1 c. heavy whipping cream

2 tbsp sugar

1 tsp vanilla extract

In a large bowl, combine heavy whipping cream, sugar and vanilla. Using a hand mixer, beat until stiff peaks form, about 5-7 minutes.

To make trifles, fill 4 bowls with a layer of cake pieces. Top with a dollop or two of whipped cream, then top with apricot slices. Repeat layering until bowl is full. Serve immediately.

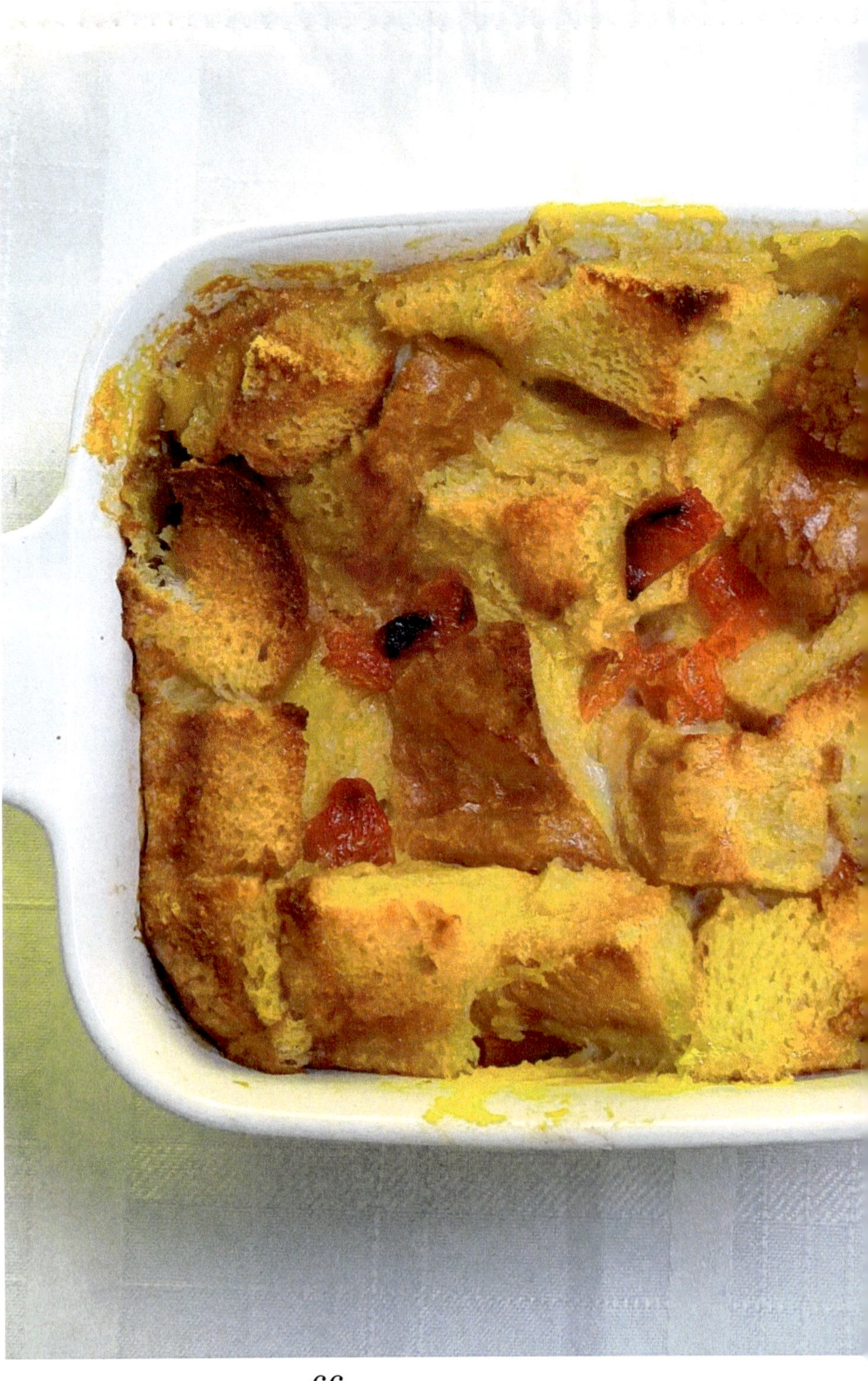

Apricot Bread Pudding

Serves 4

Time: 1 hour

Bread pudding is one of those desserts that people either love or hate. I love it, so naturally I had to make an apricot version! It's so easy and it's a perfect use of day old bread. Try it for dessert (or even better, as breakfast!)

4 beaten eggs

2 1/4 cups milk

1/2 cup sugar

1 tbsp vanilla

4 cups dry bread cubes

10 dried apricots, diced

Preheat oven to 350 F.

In a large bowl, combine eggs, milk, sugar, vanilla and dried apricots. Let soak for 5 minutes. Add bread cubes to a 2 quart baking dish, then pour egg mixture over the top.

Bake for 40 to 45 minutes until puffed up. If bread starts to get too brown, cover with foil to prevent burning.

Serve with whipped cream.

Apricot Sparkling Jello

Serves 8

Time: 20 minutes plus chilling

I love sparkling jello. There is something magical about it that I can't quite explain. The little bubbles make it so light and fluffy! It's especially good with a little whipped cream on top. Plus there are little secret orange slices in there that make it extra special. This one is great for kids, or for adults who are kids at heart.

1 c. orange juice

1 1/2 c. apricot nectar

1 can ginger ale

1 can mandarin orange slices, drained

4 packets plain gelatin

Pour apricot nectar into a large bowl. Sprinkle gelatin over apricot nectar and let rest for at least 1 minute. Heat orange juice to boiling, then pour over apricot nectar. Whisk until combined, then pour in the ginger ale. Whisk once or twice gently as to not burst all the bubbles, then pour into a glass baking dish. Sprinkle mandarin orange slices over the top, then refrigerate at least 4 hours or until set. Serve chilled.

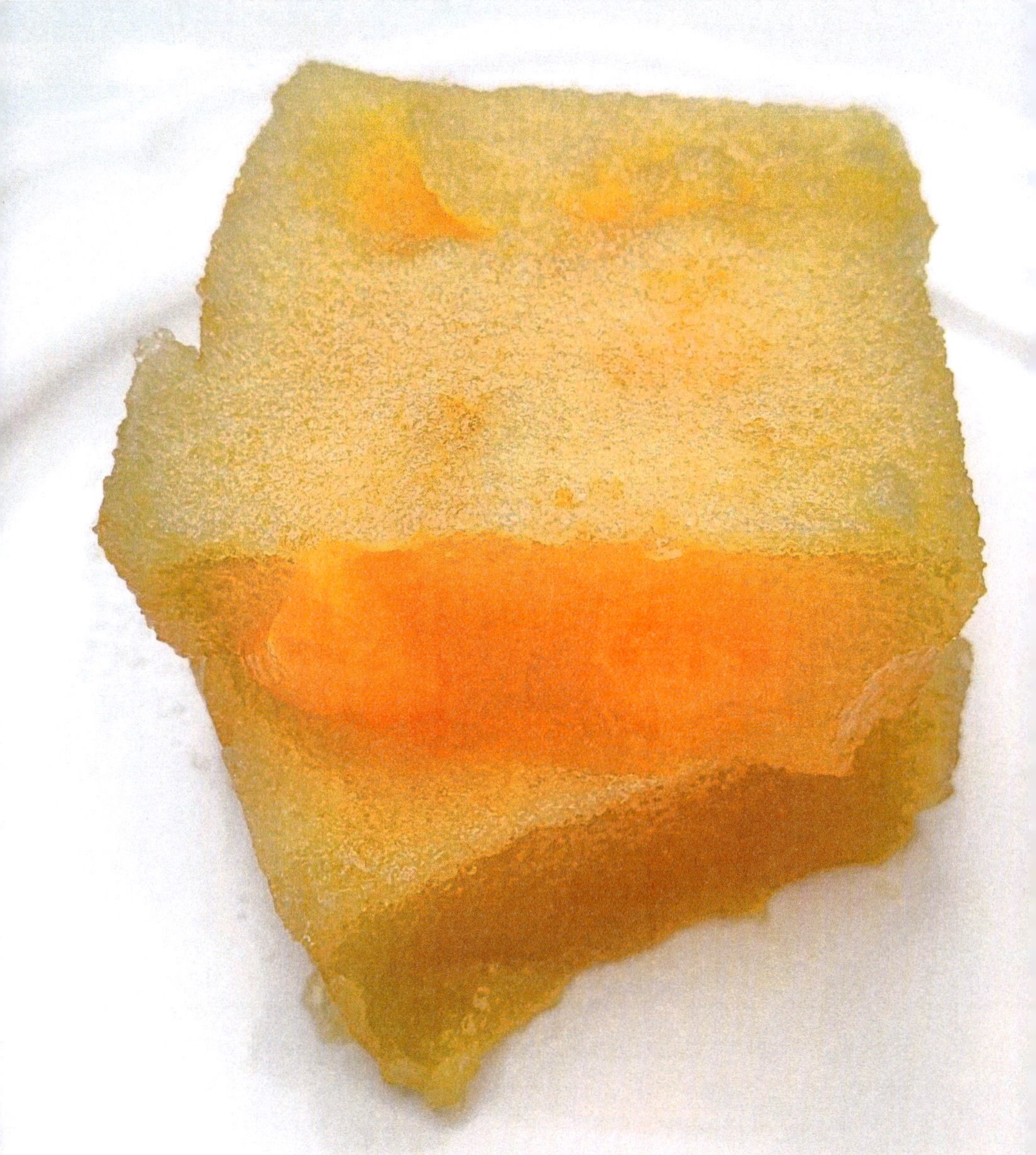

Apricot Muffins

Makes 1 dozen muffins

Time: 45 minutes

Muffins are like the perfect breakfast food. They are portable but yummy, perfect for eating on the way to work. These are definitely my best version yet! Nice a light, almost like a cupcake. But healthy enough to be called a muffin, so go ahead and eat a few for breakfast!

1 3/4 c. all purpose flour	1 tsp vanilla extract
1/3 c. sugar	1/4 c. apricot nectar
2 tsp baking powder	3/4 c. milk
1/4 tsp salt	1/4 c. vegetable oil
1 egg, beaten	8 dried apricots, chopped

Preheat oven to 400 F. Grease or line a 1 dozen muffin tin.

In a medium bowl, combine vanilla, apricot nectar, milk and vegetable oil. Add in dried apricots, then set aside.

In another bowl, combine flour, sugar, baking powder and salt. Stir to combine. Add egg to milk mixture, then add to flour mixture. Stir until just combined, then spoon into muffin tin, filling each about 2/3 of the way full.

Bake for 18 to 20 minutes or until golden and a wooden toothpick inserted in the center comes out clean. Cool for minutes then remove from muffin tin and let cool for another 10 minutes before enjoying.

Apricot Almond Bread

Makes 1 loaf

Time: 1 hour

Quick breads are a great alternative to muffins, if you are lazy like me. Sometimes scooping out perfectly portioned amounts of dough into a muffin tin is just too much for me. So I'll tweak the recipe just a little and pour it into a bread pan and voila! Bread in a snap. This one is really good heated up with a little butter on top.

- 1 3/4 c. all purpose flour
- 1/3 c. sugar
- 2 tsp baking powder
- 1/4 tsp salt
- 1 egg, beaten
- 1 tsp vanilla extract
- 1/4 c. apricot nectar
- 3/4 c. milk
- 1/4 c. vegetable oil
- 10 dried apricots, chopped
- 1/4 c. chopped almonds

Preheat oven to 400 F. Grease or line an 8" by 2" by 3" loaf pan.

In a medium bowl, combine vanilla, apricot nectar, milk and vegetable oil. Add in dried apricots, then set aside.

In another bowl, combine flour, sugar, baking powder and salt. Stir to combine. Add egg to milk mixture, then add to flour mixture. Add in all but 1 tbsp of almonds.

Stir until just combined, then pour into loaf pan. Sprinkle remaining almonds on top.

Bake for 35 minutes or until golden and a wooden toothpick inserted in the center comes out clean. Cool for 15 minutes then remove from tin and let cool for another 10 minutes before slicing. Enjoy with some butter slathered on top.

Apricot Scones with Lemon Glazed

Makes 8 large scones or 12 small scones

Time: 1 hour

Scones are so much fun to make. Simply whisk all the ingredients together, then knead the dough a few times and voila! Scones! They are even more perfect when they are glazed and this lemon glaze is perfect with the apricots. If you like your glaze on the thicker side, simply keep adding more powdered sugar until you reach the consistency you like.

2 1/2 cups all purpose flour

2 tbsp sugar

1 tbsp baking powder

1/4 tsp salt

1/3 cup butter, softened

2 eggs, beaten

1/2 cup half and half

1/4 c. apricot nectar

10 dried apricots, chopped

Glaze:

1/8 tsp lemon zest

1 tbsp lemonade

6 tbsp powdered sugar

Preheat oven to 400 F. In a medium bowl, combine half and half plus apricot nectar. Add in dried apricots and set aside.

In a large bowl, combine flour, sugar, baking powder and salt. Add in butter, then using a fork or pastry blender, cut in butter until mixture resembles coarse crumbs. Set aside.

Mix together eggs into half and half mixture, then pour into flour mixture. Stir just until moistened, then pour onto a lightly floured surface.

Knead dough 10 to 12 times to bring dough together. If making small scones, cut dough in half. Roll each half into a 6 inch circle, then cut into 6 wedges. Repeat with remaining dough.

If making large scones, shape dough into an 8" circle. Cut into 8 wedges.

Place scones onto parchment paper lined baking sheet at least 1" apart. Bake for 12 to 14 minutes until golden. Set aside to cool.

In the meantime, make the glaze by whisking together lemon zest, lemonade and 2 tbsp powdered sugar. Once powdered sugar has been absorbed, add in another tablespoon, then stir to combine. Repeat until all powdered sugar has been absorbed and no lumps remain.

To glaze scones, brush glaze on top of scones after they have cooled.

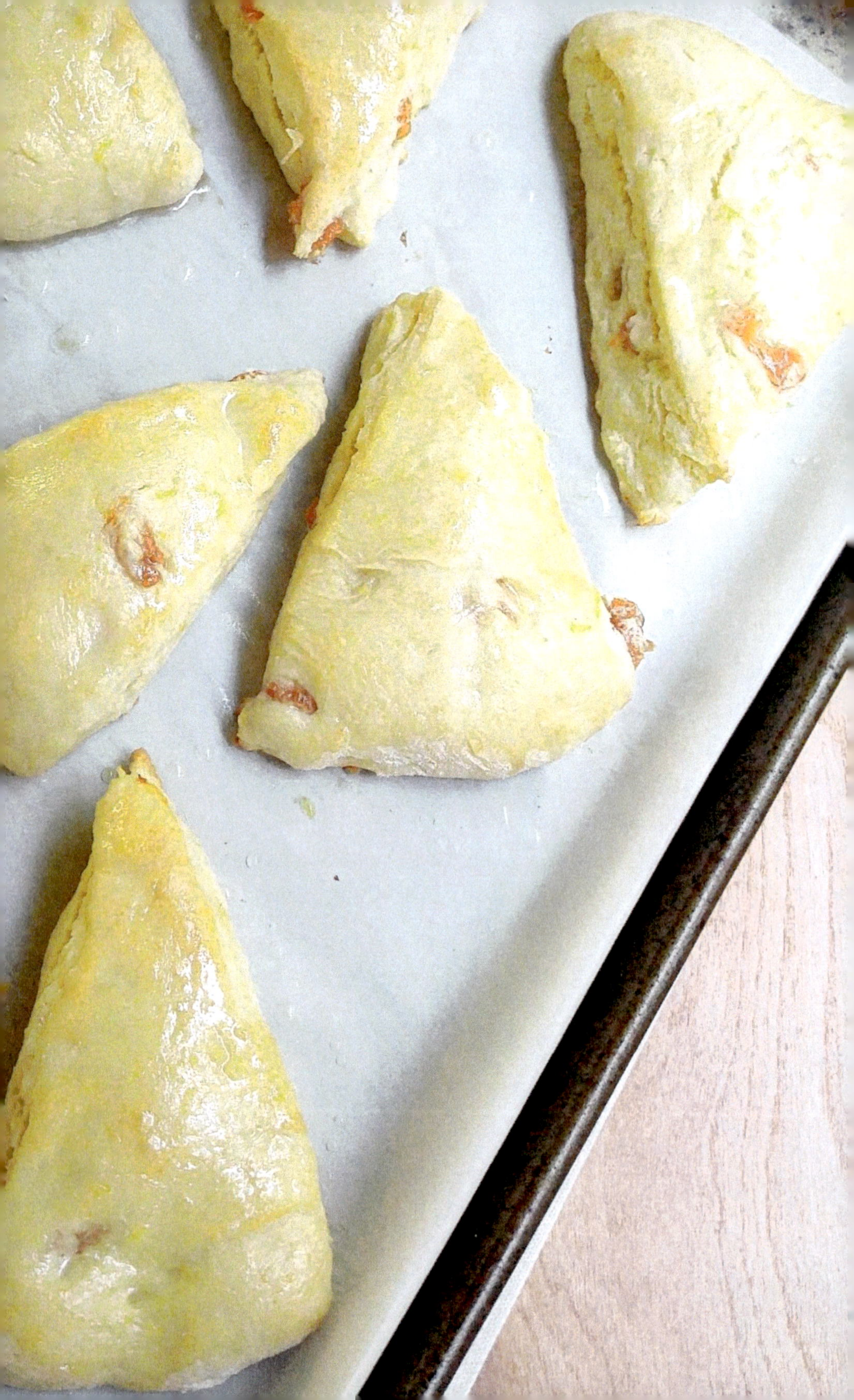

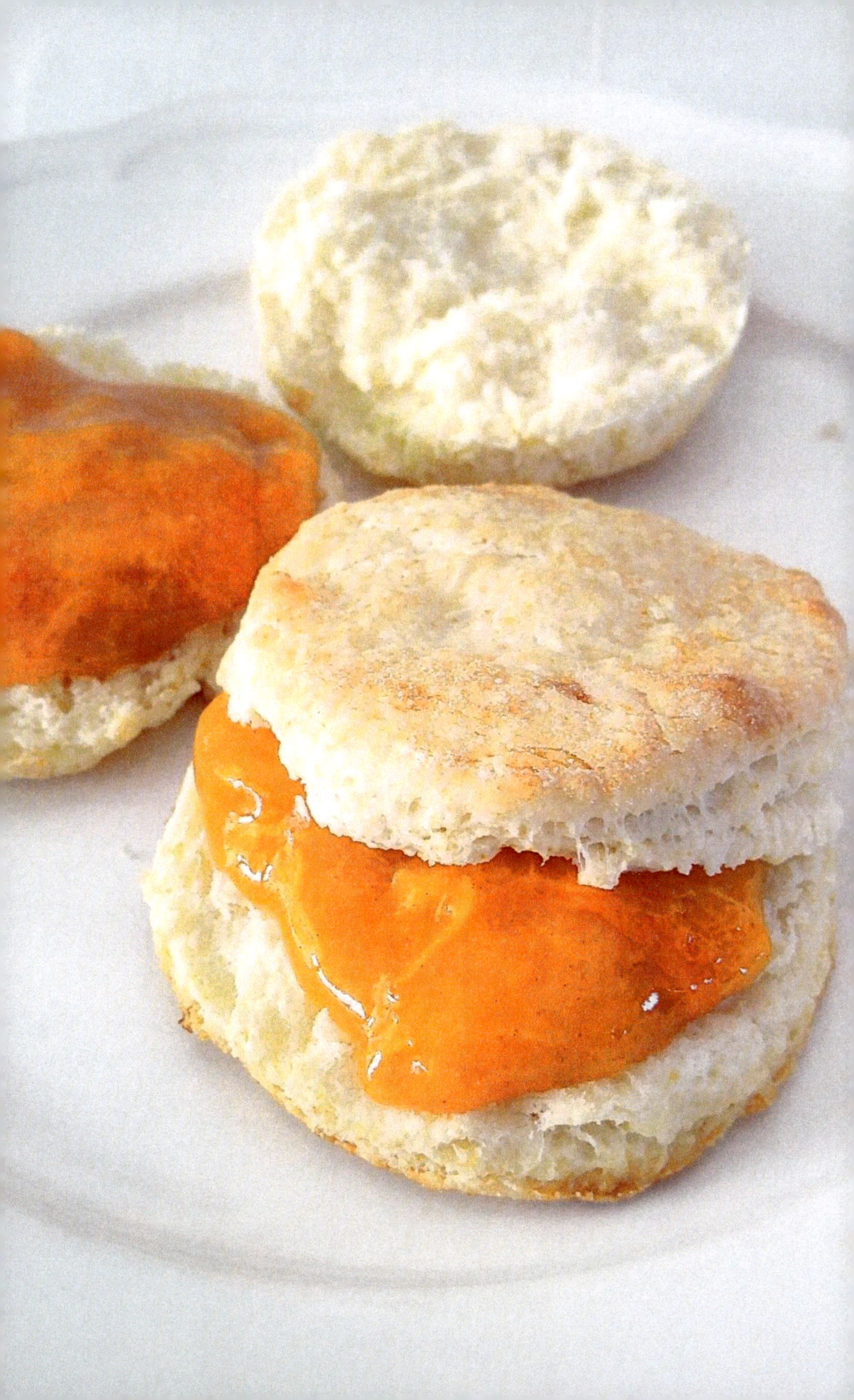

Biscuits with Stewed Chai Apricots

Makes about 1 dozen biscuits

Time: 30 minutes

Biscuits are so much fun to make! Plus they come together in a snap and are perfect for breakfast, dessert, or even as a roll to go with dinner. The stewed apricots make these biscuits a delicious sweet treat, especially when still warm from the oven and slathered in butter.

Biscuits:

2 c. AP flour
1 tbsp baking powder
2 tsp sugar
1/2 tsp cream of tartar
1/4 tsp salt
6 tbsp butter or vegan butter (I used Earth Balance)
2 tbsp vegetable shortening
2/3 c. almond milk

Preheat oven to 450 F. Combine flour, baking powder, sugar, cream of tartar and salt in a large bowl. Cut in butter and shortening with a pastry blender or two knives until butter is the size of peas or smaller. Pour all of the milk into the batter and mix together using a fork until just moistened. (There will still be some dry ingredients that don't get mixed in and that's ok).

Pour dough onto a lightly floured surface and knead 4

to 5 times just to combine the dough a little better. Roll the dough out to 1/2" thick then cut dough with a 2.5" cookie cutter. Place biscuits on an ungreased baking sheet with room between them and bake for 10 minutes or until golden brown. Let cool then enjoy.

Stewed Apricots:

2 apricots, pitted and diced

1 tbsp apricot preserves

1/4 c. apricot nectar

1 tsp honey

1/8 tsp ginger

1/8 tsp cinnamon

1/4 tsp allspice

Combine all ingredients in a small saucepan. Bring to a boil, then reduce to simmer. Cook for 10 minutes or until apricots break down. Stir to combine, then serve on biscuits.

Apricot Coffee Cake

Makes 9 servings

Time: 1 hour

Coffee cake always reminds me of something that gets served at business meetings, but it's so much better when served to loved ones. Usually you find peach coffee cakes, with a syrupy filling from a can, but this version is way better because it uses fresh apricots instead. Give it a try for a delicious weekend breakfast!

- 2 cups pitted and sliced apricots
- 1/4 c. water
- 2 tbsp sugar
- 2 tbsp cornstarch
- 1 1/2 c. all-purpose flour
- 1/4 c. sugar
- 1/2 tsp baking powder
- 1/4 tsp baking soda
- 1/4 c. butter
- 1 beaten egg
- 1/2 c. milk
- 1/2 tbsp vinegar
- 1/2 tsp vanilla extract
- 1/4 c. all-purpose flour
- 1/4 c. sugar
- 2 tbsp butter

To make the filling, combine apricots, water, sugar and cornstarch in a medium saucepan. Bring to a boil, then reduce to a simmer. Cook for 5 minutes, then set aside.

Combine milk and vinegar and set aside.

In a large bowl, combine the 1 1/2 cups flour, the 1/4 cup sugar, baking powder, and baking soda. Cut in the 1/4 c. butter until mixture resembles coarse crumbs.

Mix egg and vanilla extract into milk, then pour into flour mixture. Stir until moistened. Spoon half the batter into an 8x8x2 baking dish and spread into an even layer. Pour apricot mixture on top, and spread evenly. Drop spoonfuls of remaining batter on top.

In a small bowl, mix together 1/4 c. flour, sugar and butter to resemble coarse crumbs. Sprinkle over cake, then bake for 40 to 45 minutes until golden.

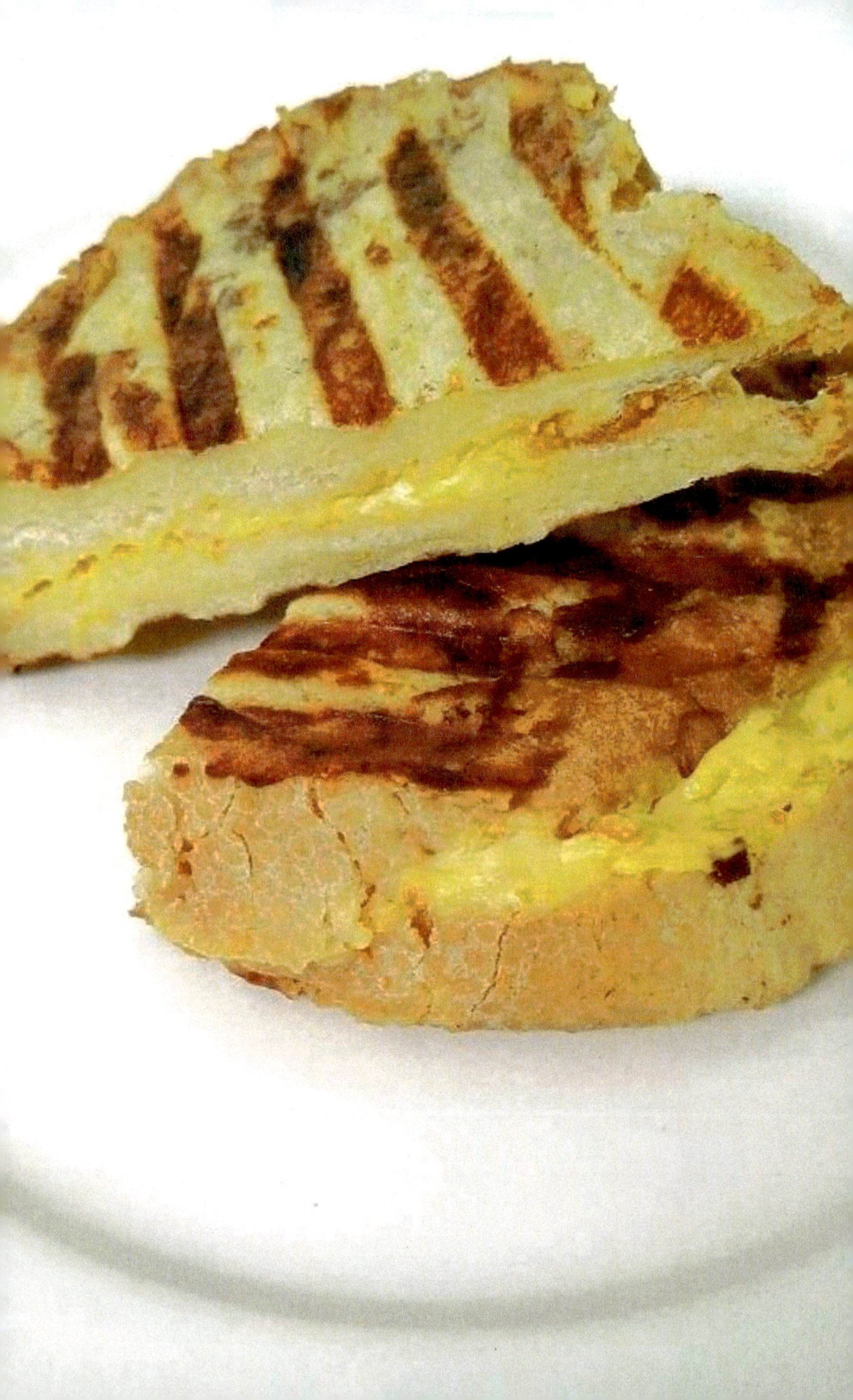

French Toast Paninis with Apricot Filling

Makes 4 sandwiches

Time: 30 minutes

I was originally going to make this as a stuffed French toast bake, but halfway through I had a lightbulb moment. Why not make these sandwiches and turn them into paninis?!?! It was probably one of my most brilliant ideas ever. These are so good I couldn't stop eating them! If you like it extra sweet, you can always dunk these in maple syrup. Or if you like them savory, add a slice of cooked bacon to each sandwich before soaking in the egg mixture.

1 French bread loaf

1 package cream cheese

1 tbsp honey

1 tbsp apricot nectar

2 eggs, beaten

1/2 c. milk

1/4 tsp cinnamon

2 tbsp sugar

Cut 8 slices of bread, each 1" thick. In a food processor, combine cream cheese, honey and apricot nectar. Process until smooth. Spread cream cheese on one side of 4 slices of bread, then top with another slice to create a sandwich.

In another bowl, mix eggs, milk, cinnamon and sugar together. Dip sandwiches into egg mixture, and let bread soak up all the egg mixture, flipping a few times to let soak evenly.

Cook sandwiches on a panini maker according to manufacturer directions. Serve hot.

Apricot Chai Spiced Pancakes

Makes about 8 pancakes

Time: 15 minutes

I love Saturday morning pancakes. Usually I stick with plain pancakes or the standard blueberry, but why not make them super special and add in some apricots and spices? Chai spices and apricots go so well together, they make for some really great pancakes. Serve hot with butter and syrup! If you are feeling really lazy, simply use your favorite pancake mix and substitute half of the milk with apricot nectar and add in the spice mixture below.

1 cup all purpose flour

1 tbsp sugar

2 tsp baking powder

1/4 tsp salt

1/4 tsp cinnamon

1/8 tsp cloves

1/4 tsp ground ginger

1/8 tsp allspice

10 dried apricots, diced

1 beaten egg

1/2 cup milk

1/2 cup apricot nectar

2 tbsp cooking oil

In a bowl, combine flour, sugar, baking powder, salt, cinnamon, cloves, ginger and allspice. In another bowl, combine egg, milk, apricot nectar, dried apricots and oil. Let stand for at least 5 minutes to let dried apricots plump up. Add egg mixture to flour mixture and stir until just combined (batter will be lumpy).

Heat a griddle pan or nonstick pan over medium low heat. Pour 1/4 cup of batter into the pan, then let cook for 2 minutes of each side. Serve warm with syrup and butter.

Vanilla Waffles with Apricot Syrup

Makes about 1 dozen waffles

Time: about 30 minutes

Waffles are so much fun! Those little pockets of dough that hold melted butter and syrup just make them so delicious. All the better to hold this amazing apricot syrup. I'm a huge fan of fruit syrups, whether its strawberry, blackberry or even marionberry. This syrup is also great on blueberry pancakes. I suggest making a double batch of the syrup if you are an avid pancake or waffle eater, like I am!

Waffles:

- 1 3/4 cups all purpose flour
- 2 tbsp sugar
- 1 tbsp baking powder
- 1/4 tsp salt
- 2 eggs
- 1 3/4 c. milk
- 1/2 c. cooking oil
- 1 tbsp vanilla

In a medium bowl, combine flour, sugar, baking powder and salt. In another bowl, beat together eggs, milk, oil and vanilla. Pour egg mixture into flour mixture, then whisk to combine until just moistened.

Pour 3/4 cup batter onto grids of a preheated waffle maker. Bake according to your waffle maker's directions. Repeat with remaining batter.

Syrup:

In a small saucepan, whisk together 1/2 cup apricot nectar, 2 tbsp sugar and 1/2 tsp cornstarch. Bring to a boil, then remove from heat and let stand until ready to use.

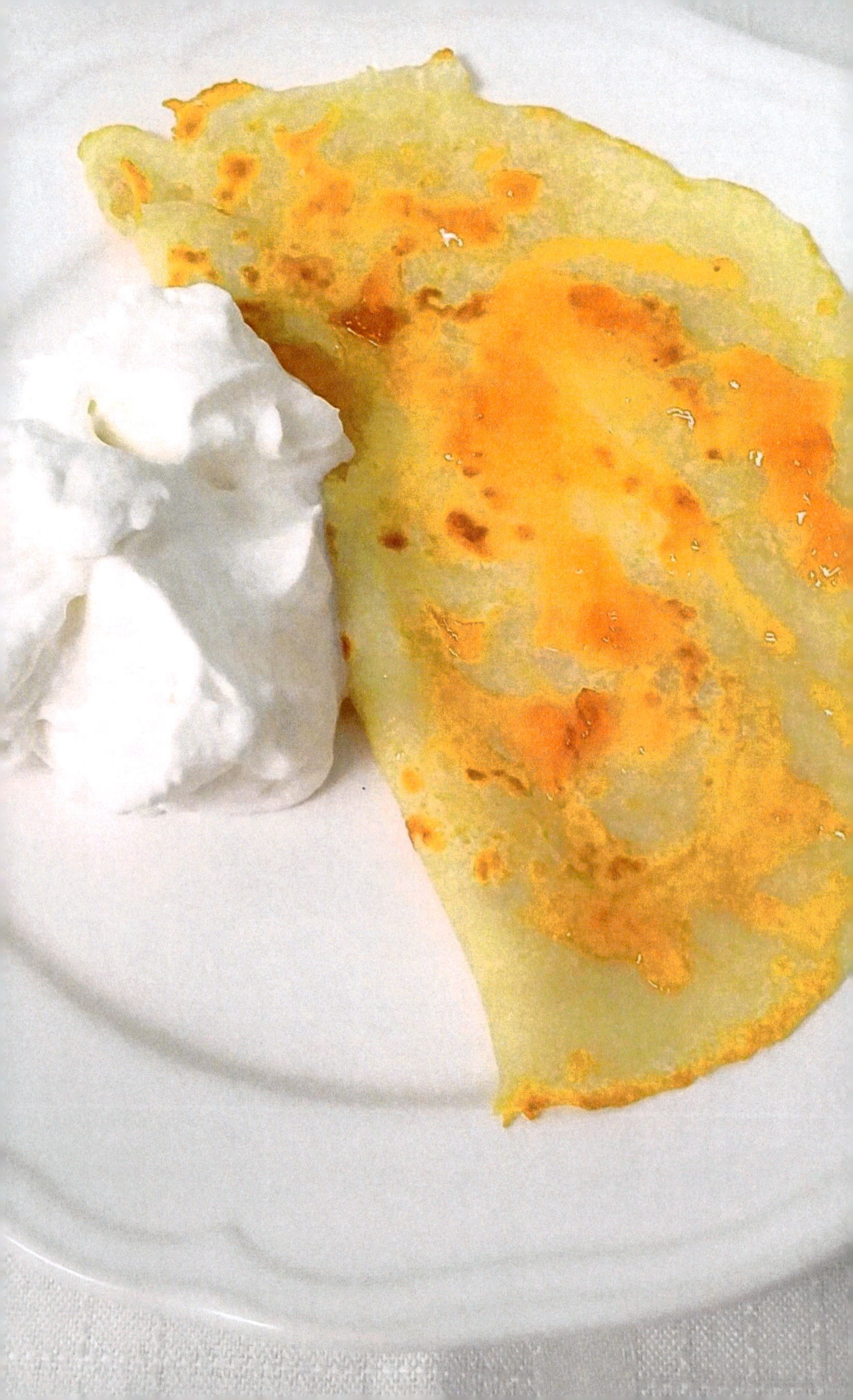

Crepes with Apricot Jam & Whipped Cream

Serves 6

Time: 30 minutes

Crepes seem difficult and fancy, but they are actually really easy once you get the hang of it. I had a French exchange student stay with me when I was a teen and she taught me how to flip the crepes in the pan, but if you aren't as talented, you can always use a spatula. The trick is to let the crepe cook until its cooked almost all the way through, then flip so the batter doesn't splatter everywhere. I decided to serve these the traditional way: with jam and whipped cream, the way they eat them in Paris.

2 eggs, beaten	1/4 tsp salt
1 1/2 cups milk	Apricot jam
1 cup all-purpose flour	Fresh whipped cream
1 tbsp oil	

Combine all ingredients in a bowl. Whisk until smooth. Let stand for 5 minutes. Heat a 12" skillet over medium low heat. Pour 2 tbsp batter into pan, then lift pan and tilt to spread batter evenly. Cook for 1 minute or until batter is cooked through, then flip and cook for 30 seconds on other side. Serve folded in half with jam spread on the top.

Final Words

I hope you enjoyed these recipes as much as I enjoyed creating them!

If you loved this book, please leave me a 5 star review on Amazon along with your comments and favorite recipes! I'd love to hear what you think of them.

Also, when you make these recipes, please tag me in them on Instagram so I can see them! You can find me at Instagram.com/huckleberryeats or use the hashtag #huckleberryeats

I'd love to connect with you on social media, too!

Facebook.com/huckleberryeats

Pinterest.com/rachelvdolek

Be sure to visit www.thehuckleberryeats.com to get more recipes, updated weekly with new deliciousness!

Thank you again for buying a copy of my book! Please share my work with all your foodie friends!

About the Author

Rachel Vdolek is an Amazon Bestselling author with over 5 published books.

She has been cooking since she was a kid, baking cookies with her Babi. She published her first cookbook in 2014 and has plans for many more.

When Rachel is not in the kitchen, she loves to ski, hike and explore the Pacific Northwest with her fiancé.

Made in the USA
San Bernardino, CA
09 August 2017